Ashley R⟨✓⟩   Y0-DBY-922

Edna Day

SAVED TO SERVE

THE STORY OF ASHLEY AND EDNA DAY

Ashley and Edna Day

authorHOUSE®

AuthorHouse™
1663 Liberty Drive, Suite 200
Bloomington, IN 47403
www.authorhouse.com
Phone: 1-800-839-8640

First published by AuthorHouse   8/1/2008

ISBN: 978-1-4389-0310-1 (sc)
ISBN: 978-1-4389-0308-8 (hc)

Printed in the United States of America
Bloomington, Indiana

This book is printed on acid-free paper.

Dedicated to our five children,
Jennifer, Alyson, Nicola, Jillian and Andrew,
all of whom love the Lord Jesus Christ
and continue to serve Him
in their own spheres of life.

Manzanita, September, 1975,
just prior to leaving for Ilfracombe, England (page 167).

Table of Contents

PREFACE

The story in this book contains nothing spectacular. It is a simple account of two people who lived, laughed, loved and served in the second half of the twentieth century. They were not famous and did not associate with famous people. They are representative of thousands of others who quietly live their lives in a changing world.

However, running beneath this everyday story is a second account which is not commonplace. It describes the way God took two ordinary people and without formal theological training placed them in a ministry that over a period of forty-five years impacted thousands of lives. It is a demonstration of what God can do if we are willing to step out in faith. The narrative takes us from a handful of folk in a country chapel to a sizable congregation in a multi-million dollar sanctuary; from a five-minute devotional on a local radio station to a Bible teaching ministry that covers much of the world. This was God's doing and it is marvelous in our eyes.

As you read these pages, think back over your own life. Will you record it for the encouragement and inspiration of the generations to follow, or will your testimony fade from history and be lost for ever? The hymn-writer wrote these words:

> "*Time, like an ever-rolling stream,*
> *Bears all its sons away.*
> *They fly, forgotten as a dream*
> *Dies as the opening day.*"

One way to avoid this tragic loss is to record your experiences on paper. Others will read them and be inspired to do likewise.

CHAPTER 1

Ashley's Story

The period between the two great wars was unique in the history of Great Britain. Queen Victoria died in 1901 and her son, Edward V11, came to the throne. The Edwardian period bridged the gap between the severe social protocol of Victorian times and the more liberated generation that entered World War 1. By 1918, when the troops came home from war, the people were ready for change. Significant events took place. Women won the right to vote and soon comprised 43% of the electorate. A greater focus on personal freedoms developed and although the Great Depression (the Slump) hit in 1929, there was steady progress in technology. Throughout the 1920s and 1930s an emphasis on individual rights gradually evolved, finding its fulfillment in the years following World War 2. This interim period was the era into which both Edna and I were born.

Welling, Kent

My parents, Harry and Minnie Day, took delivery of me on December 27th, 1928, in Bexleyheath, Kent, a suburb of southeast London. I have no personal recollection of the event but I vividly remember the house in which I gradually became conscious of being a person. It was a small semi-detached house, which my parents had purchased soon after they were married ("semi-detached", in England, is a term used for two houses joined together). Invalided out of the Royal Engineers toward the end of the First World War, my father had studied for the Civil Service examination and upon successfully passing it had landed a job at

Somerset House in London as a clerical officer in the Estate Duty office. Somerset House was then one of the central government establishments. Our house was therefore a kind of celebration. In company with perhaps fifty similar houses, it stood in a large circular street with a straight road running through its center, rather like a banjo. This center road divided the circle into two crescents and ended at a set of high park gates. Our side of the circle was named Selwyn Crescent.

Beyond the gates stretched Danson Park with old trees surrounding a large lake. Ducks waited eagerly to be fed while swans glided sedately in the deeper water, seemingly aloof from the noisy activities of their gregarious companions. The park once belonged to the manor house, which still stood grandly amid a grove of huge rhododendron bushes overlooking the lake. The park was now a public playground. To me, it was a mysterious place because I was forbidden to go there alone. My mother had warned me off in such stern terms that to do so would have been the equivalent of a trek into Outer Mongolia or an expedition to Timbuktu. I imagined being lost in there or worse, falling into the lake, though my sister had once ridden her bike into it and had come home alive.

Our house was identical to thousands built between the two great wars. The front door opened into a narrow hallway which ended at the kitchen door. A staircase on the right side took a right angle turn at the top to the landing. Downstairs, on the left side of the hallway, were two rooms. The first was known as "the best room", rarely used except when visitors stopped by, while the second was called "the dining room" because that is where the family ate their meals. Though identified with dining, this room also served as our living room. The radio was there and mother's treadle sewing machine, on which she manufactured most of her dresses. A coal fire burning in the fireplace was responsible for heating the room but the door was kept tightly closed to prevent heat escaping into other areas of the house. Consequently, the hallway and bedrooms were horribly cold in the winter. Three bedrooms and a bathroom were arranged around the upstairs landing, the third bedroom being very small and sometimes referred to as "the box room". The toilet sported a cast iron water tank, fixed to the wall above our heads, with a pipe descending to the rear of the toilet bowl. A pull chain terminating in a china handle dangled from a lever in the tank. Flushing the toilet was therefore always referred to as "pulling the chain" because that is precisely what we did.

In view of today's standards, I often wonder how we ever reached adulthood. For instance, the pipes in our first house were all made of lead, which meant that for the first ten years of my life I drank water straight out of lead pipes. In addition, all paint was made with lead and many times during our early years we chewed on things coated with it. To make matters worse, holes in the wall-plaster were usually fixed with an asbestos paste. It came in the form of powder (which rose in a cloud when you opened the packet). After being mixed with water and squeezed in the hand to form a kind of dough, it was then applied to the blemish. Pipes in most schools and hospitals were routinely encased in a thick coating of asbestos and some people even lived in cheap housing that was constructed of asbestos sheets nailed to a wooden frame. Another unrecognized hazard was mercury (quicksilver). We used to play with it at school and sometimes brought it home. It was fascinating stuff, so fluid we could not pick it up. Its shiny nature and heavy weight made it a favorite among the kids. Any of those things today would cause panic and bring men in moon suits rushing to save us from contamination. Yet we grew up normal and seem to have suffered no ill effects from our exposure to such "deadly" materials.

During the cold winter months, preparing for bed was quite a performance. There would often be "Jack Frost" on the inside of the unheated bedroom windows, making undressing there singularly unattractive. We would therefore change into our pajamas downstairs by the living room fire and then rush upstairs and jump into bed as quickly as possible. Hot water bottles were standard equipment and during periods of extreme cold we would roll ourselves in a blanket before bundling into bed, in a vain attempt to maintain the heat we had accumulated downstairs. I always associated the cold hallway with decorating for Christmas because a special feature was hung on the light fixture at the bottom of the stairs and I "helped" Dad put it up. We would freeze in the process.

My father, an avid gardener, had transformed the small lot behind the house into a place of beauty. A rectangular lawn, edged with London Pride, ended in a rockery containing a sunken fishpond. Beyond this stood a trellis screen covered with rambler roses and on the far side of the trellis fruit trees grew in profusion. A swing, which provided endless recreation for my sister and me, also occupied this area. The sound of neighbors mowing their lawns with push-mowers on summer evenings, while a soft breeze stirred the curtains at the open bedroom window, is permanently etched into my memory.

Life during those early days was pleasant and secure. As I look back, despite my memories of cold weather, the sun always seemed to shine, though I know in reality it did not. Life was regulated and secure. My father left home promptly at the same time each morning, walked to the railway station and caught the same train to London. At precisely the same time each evening he would return, providing a sense of stability to the household. We were a happy family and lived a quiet and respectable life amid neighbors and friends who co-inhabited our crescent. My mother had lost a baby boy between my sister, Audrey, and myself, leaving a gap of six years. Consequently, Audrey consistently did more adult things than I, creating a determination within me to catch her up and enjoy the same privileges, an ambition that never materialized.

I knew very little of my paternal grandparents. I remember meeting Granddad Day only once. I am told he was a signalman for the Southern railway and lived in Sydenham, a suburb in southeast London. On the one occasion when I met him he was sitting in the "best room" awaiting a cup of tea. I ventured in to look at him and he said "'Allo chum". Startled, I explained that our cat was named "Chum" and that my name was Ashley. He replied, "Well, you're my chum ain't yer?" That caused me to exit the room and I never saw him again. It was never explained to me why we saw so little of my father's parents and it never occurred to me to ask.

However, I was occasionally permitted to stay with my mother's folks in Slade Green, with whom we were much closer. This was a great joy because my granddad was a driver for the Southern Railway. Originally he had driven steam locomotives but after the line was electrified he transferred to the electric trains. Gentle by nature and possessing an acute sense of humor, he was a special attraction to me. He had a bald head which rose to a kind of bump on top. I once asked him about his bump and he told me it had been caused by someone dropping a metal ball on his head when he was young. I believed the story implicitly when I was a child, but now I doubt its veracity. I think God just made him that shape. Granddad's eyes were a sparkly blue and his big walrus mustache seemed to intensify the sweetness of his smile. He would take me over to the engine sheds and allow me to climb up into the trains and touch the levers. He would tell hair-raising stories of adventures he had had, such as clambering along the side of a locomotive at full speed to repair a faulty part. He even spoke of a crash that had occurred in the dim mists before I was born. I would sit on his lap and listen in awed silence as he used special noises to emphasize the most dramatic points of his tales. He rolled his own cigarettes which always seemed to have wet ends, with pieces of loose tobacco protruding beyond the paper. His waistcoat, adorned with a watch chain upon which hung a tiny gold compass, was often sprinkled with ash that accidentally fell from his cigarette while he spoke. I was often surprised that the whole cigarette did not fall out of his mouth but Granddad possessed a talent for sticking it to his lower lip so that however wildly it wagged up and down only the ash fell.

When he was not at work, Granddad busied himself on his allotment (a portion of land rented for the purpose of growing vegetables) or working in his woodwork shop down beside the chicken run. It had a comfortable, musty smell about it, a mixture of sawdust and old tools. Granddad enjoyed carving and boasted an extensive collection of carving chisels, which he kept razor sharp. I was not allowed to touch them but he sometimes fixed me up with a hammer, nails and some old wood, with which I made imaginary ships and airplanes.

In contrast to Granddad's easygoing nature, Grandma was a small, neat, energetic lady, with snow-white hair. Most of the time she held the deciding vote in the family, though my mother once told me that if his anger were raised (which was very rare) Granddad was definitely the head of the house. In her young days Grandma had been "in service" as cook for Lord Glenn Connor. Now she organized the household in a manner reminiscent of Mrs. Bridges in "Upstairs, Downstairs".

During one of my visits to my grandparents I remember being taken for a long walk on the Crayford Marshes. This area was not wet and soggy, as the name might suggest, though water did lie in the lower areas. It was a wild, open expanse of land bordering the Thames in its lower reaches. The sun shone when we took our walk and birds were everywhere. Larks sang in the sky above us, while pewits and curlews called from the long grass that bordered our pathway. Man-made sounds were distant and muffled. Deep in the marshes we came to an old moat-house, known as "Howbury Moat". It was built by William the Conqueror's half brother in the 12th century. It was falling into disrepair when I saw it but at one time it had been a fortified feudal retreat and had actually been occupied until the early 1930's. I remember also seeing barges with red sails moving up and down the river Thames, a scene that has now gone for ever.

School

The first carefree years of my life eventually came to an end and when my fifth birthday arrived it was time for me to start school. I was duly enrolled in Hook Lane School and taken along by my mother on the first day of term. I hated school from that day to the end of my academic career. Some children relish the opportunity to be in the company of other kids but for some unknown reason I looked upon it as a violation of my freedom and resented being forced to sit in lines and study subjects which I was convinced I would never use. From a child I aimed to be a farmer and I could see no future in speaking French to the cows.

I have few recollections of that first school. I can remember the classroom and a few of the things we did in it, but beyond that my memory is hazy. Strangely, the two events that stand out most vividly in my mind were somewhat negative in nature. On one occasion it was "Parents Night" and the children put on a display calculated to demonstrate their progress during the year. Our class was entrusted with a physical display in which the first boy ran on to the gym floor and "made a back". The second boy then leap-frogged over him and made a similar "back". The third boy leaped over both boys and repeated the stance until eventually the whole class was supposed to be leap-frogging round the gym in a light and confident manner. I was somewhere toward the back of the line and, not having been blessed with an athletic nature, I was not very good at leap-frogging. The result was that instead of clearing the boys in my path I managed to knock them all over and we ended up in a giggling heap on the gym floor. The audience laughed uproariously, the teacher was mortified and my parents embarrassed. "Why did it have to be *their* child who messed things up?" Why did it have to be *their* boy who transformed the 1st grade extravaganza into a circus?" Life is not always fair and sometimes God uses one's offspring to develop humility!

The second event that was fixed in my memory also took place when the school was entertaining the parents. We had learned to sing some songs for the "big night" and one or two of the children had been selected to sing solos. One of these was rather poor and did not possess a white shirt (which was obligatory on such an auspicious occasion). The teacher, seeing that I was wearing a clean white shirt, made me swap with the soloist, who was wearing a rather grungy-looking jersey. My parents were shocked to see me in the choir dressed in clothes that did not belong to me and demanded an explanation. I don't know what transpired between them and the teacher but I remember insisting that I had "heard something buzzing" in the jersey I had been obliged to wear. I believe my mother had mentioned fleas in passing, and never having seen a flea I was convinced these had caused the imaginary disturbance within my shirt.

At ten years of age I took an examination which miraculously qualified me to attend grammar school. In the England of the 1930s a grammar school was a private high school in which classical subjects were taught. I was duly enrolled at Dartford Grammar School and began the second phase of my education. The school was housed in a fine old building, rich with history. Oak paneling and gothic arches abounded inside, and a wealth of ivy without. Lessons continued more or less the same as at Hook Lane except that here the staff wore academic gowns. I was also introduced to science, French and prefects, none of which excited me unduly. The headmaster was a small, military man known as Major Pochin. He had a condescending manner that made one feel like a worm in his presence and as he sailed through the halls his gown seemed to billow behind him more obviously than those of lesser staff members.

One major change was that now, instead of walking to school, I rode the trolleybus. Trolleybuses were double deck electric buses that ran from current fed by overhead wires. They were very quiet and a welcome contrast to the old trams that ran on rails and made a fearful noise. Riding the trolleybus made me feel very grown up and I enjoyed climbing aboard each morning with my satchel over my shoulder. Rigid rules were fixed for those boys who rode public transportation. If the bus was crowded we were to offer our seat to any lady who was standing. Dire consequences were promised to anyone who failed to observe this courtesy because such a lapse would reflect on the good name of the school. Prefects were usually present to spot any boy who broke the rules. For this reason, we boys would head straight upstairs to the upper deck because very few ladies ventured that far. The swaying bus made mounting the stairs a little hazardous.

Life in the 1930s

Life in the 1930s was quite distinct from other eras. The mechanical age was quickly establishing itself but the sedate world it was replacing still flourished. Our milk was still brought round each morning on a horse-drawn cart and deposited on the doorstep in quart and pint bottles. The rag and bone man also made his rounds behind a horse. The animal's droppings were coveted for use on the garden. The sky was generally free from aircraft but when one was heard approaching, we ran out to watch it make its way overhead.

When we were sick, the doctor came to the house with his little black bag, full of mysterious gadgets. They made intriguing noises when knocked together while the doctor searched for things inside. Despite his accommodation in attending the sick in their homes, the doctor was looked upon with awe. Anything he said was considered to be cast in stone. Medicine was always dispensed in a bottle and taken by the spoonful. It was always red and always tasted abominable. I assumed the taste was put into the medicine deliberately as an incentive for the patient to recover quickly. The specter of a second bottle worked miracles.

There were no plastic or paper bags in which to carry away purchased articles from the stores. Purchases (other than groceries) were always wrapped in shiny brown paper, pulled from a roll behind the counter, and tied up with string. Shoe boxes made particularly delicious parcels to carry from the store. In the larger stores, money was handled by a system of overhead wires along which tiny canisters were propelled. The clerk would put your money in the canister and pull a cord that hung down from above. The canister, suspended from little wheels, would then shoot along the wire to the office, where change would be placed back in the canister and shot back again. I always dreamed of being allowed to pull the cord but the opportunity never presented itself. In other stores there was sometimes a system of compressed air. Your money would be placed in a cylinder which was propelled through a tube to the office. Your change would come back with a dull "huff" sound. I used to imagine the cylinder bursting out at the other end like a shell from a canon, but I was assured by my parents that its arrival was far more genteel.

In those days in England we worked with pounds, shillings and pence. The penny was split into four tiny coins called farthings. Two farthings made a halfpenny (or ha'penny) and two halfpennies made a penny. The penny was a large copper coin, about an inch and a quarter in diameter and it would still buy small items. We could buy a penny-worth of sweets (candies), for instance, and the shop-keeper would often give them to us in a cone-shaped paper bag, the shape of a large ice cream cone, having first scooped them from a big glass jar. The sixpence was a 1/2 inch silver coin and the shilling was about 1/4 inch larger. Twelve pennies made a shilling and twenty shillings made a pound. I remember my mother buying material to make a dress at "one-and-eleven-three" per yard. That was one shilling, eleven pennies and three farthings per yard. Money was worth much more in those days than it is now and people earned less of it. Three pounds per week was a good wage. Girls dreamed of finding "a handsome husband and a thousand a year". A man earning a thousand pounds a year was considered rich!

Because the silver coins were real silver in the early days, it was common practice to scrub them up and hide two or three in the pudding or mince pies at Christmas time. As children, we would eagerly hope that our portion held a "thrupenny bit" (three penny piece). There was great excitement when it did. I can still visualize my grandmother surreptitiously squinting beneath the covers of the mince pies before serving them, in an effort to ensure that we children "accidentally" received one containing a coin. She could never remember which ones were "loaded".

It is difficult now to imagine a world in which there were no: atomic energy, automatic transmissions, ball point pens, CDs, cell phones, computers, copiers, credit cards, dishwashers, disposable diapers, driers, faxes, freeways, microwaves, plastics, refrigerators, satellites, supermarkets, tape recorders, telemarketers, televisions, Velcro, video games, videos or washing machines. Yet people managed quite well without them and because they had never experienced today's gadgets they didn't miss them in the least.

Cornwall

Around the year 1934 my father bought a second-hand car. It was an open Jowett Tourer with leather seats that became so hot in the summer that it was a punishment to sit on them. On long journeys, the water in the cooling system, having no additives, tended to boil, especially up hills, and we had to stop periodically while it cooled. In this car we ventured on our first trip down to Cornwall for a week's vacation. Cornwall is the southernmost county of England and famous for its natural beauty. We rented a cottage, owned by a Mr. Hogg, who lived a few doors down from us in Selwyn Crescent. The cottage was a quaint old place, situated at the water's edge on the Camel estuary, opposite the ancient fishing village of Padstow. An old wooden boat, turned upside down, formed the step from the little yard to the beach and the bones of old boats protruded here and there from the sand.

On one of our visits a two-masted schooner, called "The Isabella", had been driven onto the beach by a winter storm. Now she lay helpless, tilted to one side, waiting for a high tide to lift her back into the water. She looked enormous to me but she was actually only of medium size. A rope hung from her bow and it was possible to climb this and explore the interior. She provided quite a lot of excitement during our visit.

Just as America is split into States, so counties in England have the same function. Many of these are very ancient and in times long ago some had their own king and even their own language. The Cornish language continued in common use until the late 18th century. County accents were also quite distinct. On our trips down to Cornwall in the thirties and forties we could tell which county we were passing through by the way people spoke. Today, with the universal access to television and ease of travel, county accents have become less marked. However, especially in the country districts, they still persist.

Though less than two hundred miles in length, the journey down to Cornwall lasted most of the day. The road twisted and turned through every town and village along the way. Due to the absence of passing lanes, we were often obliged to follow slow-moving trucks for many miles. When we complained about the smell coming from the truck's exhaust, my father would put it down to "crude oil". None of us knew what that was but we trusted Dad to know best. To get through London before the day's traffic built up, we set out in the small hours of the morning and picnicked in some country area when breakfast time arrived. While we did so, the traffic was so sparse that often several minutes would elapse between passing cars. Motoring was peaceful and speeds were low. 35 to 40 miles per hour was the normal cruising speed. Food breaks along the way were always fun. In those days it was popular for private individuals to serve teas in their gardens. We would sometimes stop at one of these tea gardens and enjoy fresh strawberries and cream.

Rocksea Cottage

My parents fell in such love with Cornwall that they decided to buy a property of their own there, which they did the following year. It was not near the water but was nestled in a peaceful wooded valley through which a stream flowed. The cottage was built on a rocky bank and its land sloped steeply down to the stream, which gurgled and chuckled as if happy to be on its way to the sea. From the opposite bank, meadows rose in green folds and cows grazed lazily in the lush grass. Beds of wild onions flourished in the moist soil and emitted a sweet-sour aroma into the air. In the spring, the woods became carpeted with bluebells. Primroses dotted the banks further up the hill. The sun-drenched railway cuttings were home to wild strawberries, sweet and red, while clumps of hazelnut bushes bordering the lanes produced abundant crops in the fall. Wildlife of all descriptions teemed.

I spent many hours by and in the stream (correctly named the river Allen). There was a mystery about it. In the silence it was almost as if one could hear voices as the water rushed over the stones. In places the overshadowing trees created green tunnels that promised adventure to anyone brave enough to explore them. There was a little island downstream from our property, which I used as a pirate's lair. I played there often but there were times when the imaginary voices frightened me and I "came ashore" where help was within call. Due to the age gap between Audrey and me, I spent most of my time alone, having no siblings with whom to play. The silence in that secluded spot sometimes became scary. Wearing rubber boots I was able to venture into the shallow areas of the river, to look for fish and pick up colored stones, but now and then I went too far and my boots filled with water. When that happened they had to be turned upside down and left in the sun to dry. Sometimes this process took days to accomplish.

"Rocksea", as the cottage was called, became our holiday destination for many years. It seemed to belong to a different world. The silence, broken only by the river below, or an occasional breeze in the woods above, made such a contrast to the noise and bustle of London that it became a haven eagerly sought. Mechanized farming had not yet reached Cornwall. Ploughs, harrows, binders, and wagons were all pulled by horses and many people still traveled to town in pony and trap. By this means an old neighbor used to take me on his trips to the mill along the valley to buy food for his livestock. I loved to watch the big millstones revolve as the water rushed under the wheel to provide power. In those days the countryside was totally peaceful, free from the noise and fumes generated by mechanized traffic today. The only man-made noise came from the distant steam train that occasionally pulled its two or three coaches along the twisty single line toward Wadebridge.

At the end of the lane, beside the narrow track that wound up the hill to the farm, was a ruined chapel. Billy Bray, the stormy Cornish evangelist of the early nineteenth century, had once preached there. Now the benches, windows and doors were gone and the building was used to house old farm implements. Its moldering walls were covered with ivy and a pair of big white barn owls claimed it as their home. Sometimes, at dusk, we would see them fly out, silent as ghosts, for their night's hunting, and frequently we would hear them hoot in the darkness. There was an atmosphere about the old chapel and we children never visited it alone after dark. There was no actual danger, of course, but the heavy clumps of ivy and the owls made us keep looking behind us, to make sure nobody was lurking in the shadows. During daylight hours we would sometimes play there happily, unmindful of the shadows that congregated when the sun went down.

Our first visit to Rocksea took place in the Spring. A light rain was falling when we arrived and the trees overhead dripped, making the ground moist and soft. The air was heavy with the sweet smell of decaying leaves. It was dark and entering the strange cottage was, to my seven-year-old mind, fraught with danger. Services were primitive. Water was drawn from a well down the lane while light was provided by oil lamps that shed a circle of light in their immediate vicinity but left the outer reaches of the room in shadow. Our introduction to Rocksea cottage was particularly strange because the previous owner (Mr. Polkinhorn) had sold it to my parents "as is", which amounted to the fact that the Polkinhorns had walked out leaving everything exactly as they had last used it. Cupboards and drawers were filled with their belongings and even the teacups in which they had drunk their final cup of tea prior to leaving remained unwashed where they had put them down. The furniture, all strange to us, tended to be dark in color, so there was a somewhat creepy atmosphere about the place as my father struck a match to light the oil lamp. The cottage was isolated in its little valley and we felt vulnerable as we took possession. The faint smell of kerosene and other people accentuated the feeling that we were trespassing on somebody else's property.

In addition to the four of us and a large Welsh sheep dog named Laddie, our luggage had been too much for our car to carry. It was therefore sent on ahead by train and was now waiting at the station to be collected. After settling us into the cottage, my father went to retrieve it, leaving mother, Audrey, Laddie and me sitting in the little parlor, pretending to be quite at ease. I was on the floor stroking Laddie. His big warm body was comforting and he loved to be fussed. Suddenly, a terrible change came over him. His droopy muscles tightened like steel and the hair on the back of his neck stood up like feathers. With a deep growl he stared into a recess in the corner of the room. He got up, and with stiff legs slowly approached the recess. I was not about to follow him and neither was Audrey. That left my mother who, with lamp in hand, bravely followed Laddie on his slow walk across the room. However, a few feet from the recess, he suddenly changed back into his old dreamy self and with a somewhat embarrassed expression on his face, walked back and lay down again beside me with a big sigh. Mother, on the other hand, who was left standing before the recess, found herself confronted by the shadowy figure of a man with a big black beard and moustache standing silently at the back of the recess. Scared, she raised the lamp in her hand, only to see a life-size portrait of a previous owner of the cottage! It was a false alarm but we were nevertheless happy to hear the car arrive back, bringing Dad and the luggage.

Despite our scary introduction to Rocksea, we soon grew to love it. The following morning the sun shone, the birds sang and the apprehension of the previous evening disappeared. The peace and beauty of the location and the quaintness of the cottage itself made it a haven in which we delighted to be. An old deed map, dating back two hundred and fifty years, identified the cottage as "Mifs Rowe's house". We often wondered who "Mifs Rowe" had been and what her life had been like. Visits to "her house" were the highlights of my early growing years and we were always sad when the time came to leave it and return to the city. A cold sense of restriction grew in the pit of my stomach whenever we approached London again, with its tight rows of houses and hard sidewalks.

War Declared

As war threatened, in the summer of 1939, our lives entered a new phase. My father volunteered to join the newly formed Ministry of Supply and was posted to Burton-on-Trent, in Staffordshire. Not knowing where this would lead and recognizing that our town would probably be a target for bombing should war break out, my parents sold our house in Welling and we moved to temporary lodgings in Burton. While there, we listened to the radio one evening and heard war declared by the then Prime Minister (Mr. Neville Chamberlain). That same night the first air raid siren sounded. We were scared but Dad gallantly told us that most of the noise would be caused by our own guns. That information calmed us at the time, but as I look back now I realize there were probably no guns to make any noise at that early stage in the war, and in any case the siren was a false alarm.

The outbreak of hostilities made Dad's position even more uncertain, so Audrey and I were sent down to Rocksea in the care of our grandparents, while our parents became more established. Granddad, a true countryman at heart, loved Rocksea and thoroughly enjoyed his stay there. It was a beautiful Fall and we spent many happy evenings with the kids who lived on the farm above our cottage. There were four of them, ranging in age from seventeen down to about eleven. The eldest, named Archie, had taken a liking to my sister and had begun to invent ways of "accidentally" seeing her. His father kept two big work horses named Tagger and Lil to do the farm work, and in the evenings Archie would bring them all the way down past our cottage to pasture them in the hope of seeing Audrey. She fell for him and on one occasion asked me if I could secure a lock of his hair. When I asked him for the favor he grinned and snipped a lock from Tagger's tail. Upon receiving it Audrey expressed surprise that Archie's hair was so coarse! Not to be outdone, I fell in love with Jean, Archie's sister, but at ten years of age one is never taken very seriously in such matters. Audrey and Archie, on the other hand, were eventually married in Liverpool.

One late summer evening during that time we kids built a kind of fort in a straw rick (stack) out in a field, and lay around in it watching the moon rise. It was a harvest moon and its soft light, coupled with the scent of new straw, created an unforgettable atmosphere. There were seven of us in all, plus a whippet dog named Nip, whose back legs trembled incessantly. Eric, Archie's younger brother (who was later shot down over Germany and killed) held Nip on his lap and sang to him in a loud off-tune voice. Eric was hopelessly tone deaf but that didn't stop him singing when he felt the urge. For his part, Nip seemed completely unaware that Eric rarely hit the note. He sat there calmly, his ears twitching occasionally when the "music" became too loud, and his back legs trembled with excitement. Jean was with us and I would have liked to sit next to her but someone else grabbed the place and I didn't get my wish. I had to be content to sit near her. It was an idyllic evening but was partially spoiled by the fact that our grandmother became alarmed by our absence and was grumpy by the time we returned home, rather late.

I had a special feeling for Eric because he once saved my life. It seemed so unfair that he should save my life and then lose his own, but it sometimes seems to work out that way. The incident occurred when I was about nine years old and playing with the farm kids on the railway track. That sounds dangerous but trains passed very infrequently on that sleepy single line, and we could usually tell when one was approaching by placing our ear on one of the rails. In that way a train could be detected a considerable distance away. We liked to put pennies on the rail and watch the train squash them to twice their size.

However, on this particular occasion we were caught unaware. We were in a deep cutting, its rock walls rising high above us, too steep to climb, when suddenly a train came round the bend. There was nowhere to go.

Some of the kids went to one side and others ran to the other. I was not sure where to go and at the last minute, in fright, I attempted to run across the rails to the opposite side. This would have proved fatal. It was then that Eric grabbed me and pressed me hard against the cutting wall. The train went by, seemingly only inches away, in a great cloud of steam and smoke, the ground trembling under its weight. Its heat, together with a wild rush of air, enveloped us but none of us was hurt. Undoubtedly, Eric saved my life that day.

Harwell, Berkshire

After some weeks, we received word from our parents that we were to join them again. By this time my father had been transferred to Didcot, in Berkshire, and had secured a house in the old-world village of Harwell. We were excited when we left the train at Reading because our new home promised many surprises. It was a rambling 17th century house, with oak beams, crooked walls and a long history. The story goes that when workmen were renovating the house they found a Roundhead helmet half-way up one of the chimneys. Presumably, its owner had either been extremely tall and had stood in the fireplace to ease his back, or he had been hiding from Royalist troops during the civil war of the 1640's. The second theory was almost certainly the correct one. Needless to say, my youthful imagination was fired by the story. I became alternately a Roundhead and a Cavalier and fought many a battle on the back stairs, defending my bedroom from invasion.

The house itself, though exciting to me, must have been a nightmare for my mother. The floors were made of stone slabs and every room was on a different level. Two staircases led to different parts of the upstairs and a whole family of drafts haunted its passages. Due to the slope of the bedroom floor, my parents' bed had to be kept level by placing wooden blocks under the foot. For my part, not discerning adult cares, I loved the house and everything about it. I loved the smell of the old beams, the huge fireplaces with inglenook seats hidden inside them, the wide chimneys up which young boys once climbed to clean, the twisty passages and the crazy walls. It was like living on a movie set!

Harwell itself was a picture-book village. Narrow streets and ancient houses seemed to have tumbled higgledy-piggledy out of some giant's basket and remained where they landed. The village was situated on the edge of the Berkshire Downs, a chain of high chalk hills, across which runs the Icknield Way. This is a prehistoric pathway, already ancient when the Romans came, that winds its way along the chalky spine of England from Buckinghamshire to Norfolk. It is the oldest track in England. Dotted along it are many archeological remains and in the chalky soil all kinds of fossils may be found. I have a fossil sea bun that I picked up high on the downs, indicating that this area was at one time under water. A friend of mine at school unearthed a beautiful basalt stone axe head, made by prehistoric hands. This was intriguing, not only because of its rarity as an artifact but because basalt is not found in that part of the country. In those days, Harwell was in Berkshire, where it had been for hundreds of years, but in 1974 the authorities decided to move the ancient boundaries. Today the village is considered to be in Oxfordshire.

Down in the village, the grocer, baker and butcher were all like characters out of a Dickens novel. The village doctor was a distinguished, virile man of great age. He did his rounds on foot with his white hair blowing in the breeze. I dreaded going to his office because he kept a collection of amputation saws hanging on the wall for decoration. I would sit there and imagine him sawing off people's legs in the next room, a prospect that did little to ease my symptoms. He was obviously not an expert in psychology but in those days doctors did not have to be. Their patients rarely questioned their wisdom.

To me, the most exciting fact was that on the level ground just above the village, was an operational airfield, where Wellington bombers stood ready for action. Most of the airmen were members of the New Zealand Air Force. On many an evening we sat at the big round table in the dining room with a group of young men in air force blue sharing what food we had. Christmas was a special time because some of the air force boys would join us. The house was a great place in which to play "murder" or "sardines". Sadly, some of the young men ate their last meal there in our dining room. Later they took off into the night on a raid and never returned.

As I look back now, I wonder how housewives managed to so consistently put food on the table. Rationing was strict and some of the commodities needed in the kitchen were difficult to find. As a boy, I was hungry most of the time, as boys usually are, but I never went without a meal. I do remember that some meals were rather simple but they were satisfying and I never felt deprived.

Wallingford

Unfortunately, school intruded into my life, even in a lovely place like Harwell. Soon I was enrolled at Wallingford Grammar School, where the grind of classes and homework continued. The saving grace was that in order to reach Wallingford I had to follow a somewhat complicated route, which tended to ease the monotony. First, I rode my bike the three miles from Harwell to Didcot station. Then I caught the mainline train to Cholsey, where I changed to the local Wallingford line. This routine gave me many opportunities to see truly great locomotives, which I looked upon as living creatures, breathing out fire and steam and exuding an aura of immense power. Sometimes we would miss our train and have to wait for the next. That would make us late for school but it also provided a great opportunity to watch trains. My name being Day, the kids naturally called me "Daysie", which of course sounded the same as "Daisy". I sometimes noticed passengers on the train smirking into their newspapers when I was referred to as "Daysie" by the other boys. Nobody less like a "Daisy" could have been found. Wallingford provided my first and only experience of sharing a school with girls. It was a new experience which older boys would have relished but at eleven years of age one's later instincts are still in the process of surfacing and I missed out on much of the fun.

Life on the Didcot-to-Reading line was not without its memorable times. Among the gang of children who rode the train each day was an older girl named "Rosie". Rosie was a plump young lady with a round face and motherly disposition. She insisted on calling me "little one", which wounded my masculine pride. Despite my attempts to make her quit, she persisted in using that term to the end. One day I was late arriving at the station and rushed onto the plat-

19

form just as the train was pulling out. The kids all gathered at the windows and shouted encouragement for me to jump on. The noise was deafening. A porter, seeing the situation, picked me up and ran along beside the train with me. Rosie opened her door and shouted in a very loud voice, "Come on, Little One! Come on, Little One! You can do it, Little One!" However, as the train gathered speed I drew back and the porter, realizing the case was lost, put me down. I have a vivid memory of standing on the platform watching the train draw away with Rosie leaning far out of the window, waving her hand and shouting, "Good bye, Little One! Good bye Little One! Good bye Little One! Good bye Little One. . . . ." until she disappeared into the distance in a cloud of steam. Ever since then, I have nursed a secret dread of being left behind!

I imagine weather plays a role in most of our childhood memories. One that stands out in my recollection involved a day of snow. Our particular corner of Berkshire was not considered to be a snowy area but there was one year when the snowfall was particularly heavy. School was cancelled and we boarded the train back to Didcot rejoicing. There must have been freezing rain as well because as I walked home to Harwell, pushing my bike, the land seemed to be enchanted. Every stalk of grass, every twig, every dried head of Queen Ann's Lace beside the road was encased in ice. A fairy-like tinkling could be heard as the breeze caused the grasses and branches to touch one another. I picked specimens to take home but was disappointed when the icy coating either melted or fell off. They were so beautiful that I remember wishing that they could be preserved for future generations.

School meals were not particularly appetizing and occasionally I was given some money to visit a little restaurant down the road. To me this was the height of achievement -- to actually sit at my own table and order a mixed grill from a real waitress! The experience was especially rewarding when I saw members of the teaching staff doing the same. On one occasion I even saw the head master there. I felt adult, emancipated and excited all at once, though it was rather an anticlimax when, at the end of the meal, I had to return to the classroom and submit to the routine of lessons once again.

War Time Activities

Thankfully we were spared the ravages of the blitz in our peaceful village but there were some exciting moments. The airfield was bombed a couple of times, which shook us and our house considerably. Next morning we boys hurried up the hill to see Wellington bombers on fire and extensive damage to the airfield itself. We also explored some big bomb craters which impressed us greatly. On one occasion we were able to gape at a German bomber that had been brought down the previous night. We wanted to climb inside but were prevented from getting too close by armed guards who kept watch beside it. This was exciting -- real smoke, real fire, real bombs! It was the stuff films were made of! The fact that men had probably been hurt in the attack was strangely unreal to our young minds. The grim reality of it hovered only dimly in our thoughts and subconsciously assumed the same nature as Walt Disney cartoons, where characters are subjected to the most violent actions but are never really hurt. As children, we were scared of being hurt and scared of the noise. But when the event was over and the danger had gone away, it became an adventure to get as close as possible to where the action had taken place. One of my boasts was that on one occasion, hearing a bomb leave an aircraft overhead, I jumped out of bed, ran downstairs and took cover before it hit the ground! Nobody else seemed very impressed but I thought it was rather a spectacular achievement.

My father was a volunteer fire-watcher (people who kept alert for possible incendiary attacks) and on a couple of occasions he allowed me to go on patrol with him. The steady throb of aircraft overhead in the darkness indicated that London was in for a big raid again. We could always tell the difference between the sound of German aircraft and that of our own. Their engines had a different rhythm that was unmistakable.

The night sky in those days was always lit by searchlights. Their powerful beams looked like silver pencils as they searched the darkness for enemy aircraft. The lights were usually manned by ATS girls, who did a masterful job. Many paid for it with their lives because enemy aircraft would fire down the beams in an effort to put them out. If one team found a quarry, other searchlights in the vicinity would immediately join it. Together they would hold the aircraft in their beams until night

21

fighters or anti-aircraft guns could strike. Sometimes we would see the drama played out, though I never actually saw an aircraft destroyed.

Oblivious to the concern of our parents, who listened to the BBC news each evening with heavy hearts, my eleven-year-old friends and I lived our days in a make-believe world. We collected pieces of shrapnel, spent bullets, cartridge cases, pieces of aircraft, bomb fins and anything else that identified us with the struggle. It was exciting to be surrounded by servicemen of many nationalities and we imagined ourselves as being part of the action. The sky was busy with planes of all shapes and sizes. Spitfires, Hurricanes, Wellingtons, Lancasters and training planes were all familiar visitors. They gave us a kind of warm, protected feeling, which was false because, unknown to us, England was actually in a very perilous position during that phase in the war.

The radio became one of the most important items in the house. We children had to sit quietly while the news was on, in case something important was missed due to our chatter. Every evening there would be news of the war's progress on land and sea. They would report on RAF raids over Frankfurt, Hamburg, or Essen the previous night, together with the number of our planes missing. There would also be reports of raids on England and the number of enemy planes shot down. I suspect these numbers were exaggerated just a little to boost morale. Before the news each evening the BBC played the national anthems of all the allied nations, including those in occupied Europe. We came to know them quite well.

In those days, a company of "The Boys' Brigade" was formed at our church. I was not old enough to join it but an activity for the younger kids called "The Life Boys" was also organized. We wore sailor hats and navy blue jerseys, with brass badges in the form of a life belt pinned to our chests. I remember one occasion when a party was arranged. Lots of "goodies" were provided and, like all boys, we ate our fill. However, there was one boy who was evidently not well fed at home. Noticing strange bumps on his torso, a leader lifted his jersey and found several jam buns stuck to his bare tummy. He was carrying supplies home!

Around that time I organized "The Boys Home Guard". My plan was that if the Germans came we would fill empty bicycle pump tubes with sand. By swinging the pump case violently, the sand would be propelled into the enemy's eyes and while they were recovering we would dispatch them with hammers, clubs or anything else that came to hand. It all seemed perfectly logical to us (and extremely exciting) but when informed of our daring and gallant scheme, my Dad asked, "What do you think the Germans will be doing while you are charging them with the sand?" In our minds, the remark was typical of an adult, who was so logical that imagination was eclipsed! After that incident our plan lost some of its zip and the "Boys Home Guard" eventually disintegrated. Fortunately, the Germans never came and our scheme remains unproved to the present day.

On another occasion I decided to make a bomb. There was nothing scientific about my plan. I just wanted something to go "bang". I owned a half-burned-out German incendiary bomb that I had scrounged from another boy. I swapped it for something but I can no longer remember what it was. I do remember that my mother had not been at all happy when I brought it home. First I tried to get the bomb going again with matches but was disappointed. Fortunately, the magnesium that made up the main part of the bomb would not ignite. Then I scraped explosive from it and dropped the powder into an empty cartridge case. After closing its open end with pliers I hit it with a hammer. I still have the scar where a piece of the casing gouged a hole in my knee. The Lord was gracious in not making it my eye. I learned that day that you don't stand too close to home-made bombs of any variety, especially the kind you have to hit with a hammer to detonate!

Enlarged Family

As 1940 drew on, the London blitz intensified and part of our extended family suffered considerable damage to their homes. Due to the extreme danger it was agreed that they should come and live with us in Harwell. Although we had five bedrooms and three living rooms, an influx of these proportions created a certain amount of confusion. In response to our invitation, my grandparents, two aunts and two cousins all arrived one day and a great amount of shuffling took place. One aunt and her two children (one of whom was a baby) took over Audrey's bedroom and Audrey took over mine. I had nowhere to take over and ended up in Mum and Dad's room behind a screen. This was not ideal but in war time one had to adapt (so they told me). My grandparents and another aunt occupied the remaining two bedrooms and one of the downstairs rooms became their living quarters. There was only one kitchen, so some kind of an agreement had to be worked out for its use. This process was not on my wavelength and to this day I have no idea what the arrangement was, though I never witnessed any friction.

One of my aunts, being single, had to find employment. Until the outbreak of the war she had worked for Burroughs Welcome, the drug company in Dartford, Kent, but now she had no means of support. However, she soon secured a job at the ordinance depot in Didcot, where both Dad and Audrey now worked. We lived about three miles from the depot and she had to walk both ways every day because she never learned to ride a bicycle. On one occasion, feeling sorry for her plight, Audrey and I decided to teach her to ride. With the stupidly of youth, we got her mounted and then pushed her off down a hill. She yelled, "I'm going, I'm going, I'm going" and then collapsed in a tangled heap in the hedge. Luckily she was not hurt but she never went near a bicycle again, preferring to trudge to work on foot each morning.

Bicycles were the accepted means of transportation during the war. Fuel for private cars was strictly limited and only government approved vehicles were on the road. Bicycles proliferated in great numbers and people, like my aunt, who could not ride a bike, were reduced to traveling on foot. The night hours were particularly hazardous in those days. Due to the blackout, all vehicles had metal disks fixed to their headlights with slits cut in them to allow some light to escape. Above the slits were attached tiny hoods, to prevent what light there was from being seen from the air. Traffic therefore moved slowly after dark because drivers found it difficult to see where they were going. In addition, you had to know how to get to your destination because all sign posts had been removed from intersections and railway stations. This precaution was in case of an invasion. After all, there was no sense in telling the enemy where he was.

My grandfather loved the country and relished his time in Harwell. Soon he found some cronies in the village and spent many hours swapping stories with them about bygone days. During World War 1 he had been a St. John's Ambulance man and had learned a lot of first aid. One day in Harwell, he fell off the back of a cart and hurt his leg. Somebody got hold of a stretcher and they placed him upon it. I can see him now, with perspiration standing on his forehead from the pain, sitting up on the stretcher and saying, in a commanding voice, "Front man start off with the right foot and back man start off with the left foot!" It was probably good advice but it sounded humorous under the circumstances. It reminded me of a picture I had once seen of an Indian dignitary being carried on a litter by slaves.

Two Kings

Not all my experiences in Berkshire were connected with the war. For instance, one summer afternoon I was riding home from the station on my bicycle. The sun was shining warm on the quiet country road which led to the village and the smell of new-cut hay was heavy in the air. It was one of those peaceful, balmy days, which we all hold dear in our memories. After a while, something unusual caught my attention. Along the road, about a quarter of a mile ahead came a beautiful black car. It was a Rolls Royce and it sparkled in the sunshine. Reflections from the overhanging trees slipped across its polished hood and canopy as it moved quietly toward me. As it drew nearer it slowed to a crawl and I steered close to the side of the road to allow it to pass. The person in the back seat leaned forward with a sweet smile and waved to me as he went by, and in a warm flash of recognition, I found myself looking into the face of the king! The car didn't stop and soon it had disappeared round the next bend, but in those few seconds a young boy on a lonely country road had enjoyed the smile of his sovereign, a smile which was intended all for him! The remainder of the journey was covered in no time. My legs seemed twice as strong as usual and the wind which blew against me had no power to hold me back. I wanted to tell the good news to everyone. I had met the king and he had smiled at me!

That story is a beautiful illustration of another. We attended a small church in Didcot where my father was the secretary. My record in Sunday school was by no means good. In fact, I held the doubtful distinction of being the only boy in the church's history to have been physically ejected for disrupting the class. Sitting in Sunday School always seemed to be such a waste of a good afternoon. My teacher was therefore not delighted to have me in his class but he was faithful to his calling and never wavered in his determination to instruct us in the things of the Lord. One Sunday he taught on Matthew 24:36-42. The verses read like this:

"But of that day and hour no one knows, no, not even the angels of heaven, but My Father only. 37 But as the days of Noah were, so also will the coming of the Son of Man be. 38 For as in the days before the flood, they were eating and drinking, marrying and giving in marriage, until the day that Noah entered the ark, 39 and did not know until the flood came and took them all away, so also will the coming of the Son of Man be. 40 Then two men will be in the field: one will be taken and the other left. 41 Two women will be grinding at the mill: one will be taken and the other left. Watch therefore, for you do not know what hour your Lord will come."

I had seen this passage several times before but as the teacher spoke, his words took on a new authority. I knew if the Lord were to return that day my parents and sister would be taken but I would be left behind. The lesson closed and we went home. Sunday school in those days was held at 2:00 pm in the afternoon.

The truth of the teacher's words haunted me for the remainder of the day and I knew what I had to do. After the evening service I sought out the pastor. For privacy he took me into the church kitchen and there among the pots and pans he knelt with me and I received Jesus Christ as my Savior. Sadly, that had been the teacher's last Sunday before moving to another area. I never saw him again, and to my knowledge he never knew on this earth that he had been used by the Lord to gather me into the fold. No doubt he was very surprised when he reached Heaven to discover that his most pigheaded student had actually been listening to his lesson. That was the second king I met that summer but He was infinitely more important than the first!

I wish I could claim that my heart was dramatically changed and from that day onwards I lived an exemplary Christian life. Unfortunately, that was not so. I did nothing outrageous but throughout my teen years I was indifferent toward the things of the Lord. I attended church regularly, sang in the choir, won prizes in Scripture exams, was later even baptized at the Baptist church in Waterloo, but all without enthusiasm. It was not until my twenty-second year, after I was discharged from the army, that the Lord began to work on me and give me a desire to grow. I do not believe we choose the time when a zeal for the Lord is generated in our hearts. It is something He does within us. As I look back over the years I can see clearly that every step, every turn of the way, every life-changing decision was initiated by God. It seemed at the time that I made the decisions myself but hindsight is more accurate than foresight and now I can see that the Lord was leading all the way.

Turn for the Better

In June, 1941, Hitler invaded Russia and some of the pressure was taken off Great Britain. The fear of invasion was lessened and we were able to sleep more peacefully in our beds. While the full might of the German Wehrrmacht had been concentrated only thirty miles away across the English Channel, the threat of an attack had been very real, but when Hitler turned his attention to the Soviet Union we knew the threat had been removed, or at least, greatly lessened. Soon the Battle of Britain drew to a close as Hitler withdrew his bombers in preparation for his assault on Russia. The heavy bombing ceased but Doodlebugs and V2s continued to fall on London. They did not create the same destruction as the conventional bombing had done. Doodlebugs were small pilotless flying bombs that were sent put-putting across the English Channel under their own steam. When their fuel ran out they fell indiscriminately into whatever was below. They could be seen and heard approaching so their arrival was not a surprise but the damage and suffering they caused was considerable. Over six thousand civilians were killed by the V1s, and many more injured. These were followed later by the V2 rockets, which carried much larger warheads and fell without warning. They were neither seen nor heard until they exploded with a powerful and destructive force. Due probably to the late date of their introduction fewer people (about 2,700) were killed by the V2s. Londoners became used to both weapons and although careful about where they or their children went, they contrived to live almost normal lives.

When things quieted down in London, our guests decided to return home. At first it was strange without them but we soon grew re-accustomed to the extra space. Audrey claimed back her bedroom and I claimed back mine. I am sure my mother felt less strain as our home returned to its normal quiet routine.

Liverpool

I would have liked our time in Harwell to have lasted indefinitely, but Dad was in government service and every time promotion came along he was posted to a new location. One day he came home and announced he had been posted to Liverpool in Lancashire. It was bitter news. We loved Harwell, the house, the county and the people. The thought of leaving it all to go up north produced a deep ache in our hearts. There was nothing we could do to change the situation, however, and the day came when we said goodbye to our familiar and loved surroundings and boarded the train for Liverpool.

Our new home was in Great Crosby, a suburb just north of the city. It was a conventional semi-detached house, much larger and better equipped than our old house in Selwyn Crescent but a semi-detached house nevertheless. It stood in the inevitable row of identical suburban homes, surrounded by concrete sidewalks and tiny gardens. I hated it on sight, especially since we arrived three days before our furniture and had to sleep on the bare floor until it arrived. Liverpool had been badly hit during the blitz and every window in the house had been painted with a kind of shatter-proof glue. While we were waiting for our furniture to arrive we busied ourselves with razor blades, laboriously scraping it off. It was a miserable task but the ability to see through the windows was a decided improvement. It was winter and the weather was cold. Fog hung around and the atmosphere was made drearier by ships sounding their horns out in the Mersey estuary. Being a naval port, the docks were always filled with ships. Destroyers, cruisers, battleships and aircraft carriers all docked there for repairs. We saw some with great holes in their sides and wondered how they were able to stay afloat long enough to reach port. The sound of shipping created a mournful atmosphere, especially on foggy winter days.

Although by that time the bombing of England had ceased, the war continued to rage. Allied forces were fighting their way up the Italian peninsular with fearful losses and Nazi U-boats infested the waters around England. Shipping approaching or leaving Liverpool was in constant danger of attack. Ships gathered together in large convoys for mutual protection and support. We could stand on the beach at Crosby and see them gathering on the skyline, ready to leave for their distant destinations. Sometimes ships were torpedoed almost within sight of land. On one occasion I remember going down to the beach and seeing thousands of grapefruit bobbing in the water and covering the shore. A ship bringing supplies to England had been sunk and men had given their lives in the icy waters off Liverpool in their attempt to reach us. After that I never ate anything that was not produced in England without visualizing the grapefruit bobbing on the water in Liverpool Bay.

Waterloo-With-Seaforth

Once we were settled in Crosby, school demanded attention as usual and I was enrolled at Waterloo-With-Seaforth Grammar School. At first it was difficult for me, a southerner, to adjust to North Country ways, but before long I was happily speaking with a broad Lancashire accent and nobody could tell the difference between me and the natives.

One of the things that stand out most forcibly about Waterloo Grammar School was the gas mask drills. Throughout the war years it was the law to carry a gas mask wherever we went and the school staff took it upon themselves to test these contraptions periodically. We would all file down into the air raid shelter and put on our gas masks. The teacher would then come round and place a piece of card over the nozzle of each one to ensure that the face piece was airtight. We soon discovered that by blowing instead of sniffing when she or he administered the card we could make a deliciously rude noise out of the side of the mask, which we did on a regular basis. The teacher would get cross and that made us laugh all the more. Laughing inside a gas mask is a very interesting phenomenon. The sound is hilarious and when thirty kids all got the giggles inside their masks it produced an unforgettable effect.

Corporal Punishment

Corporal punishment was still in vogue at that time. Nobody, including the kids, complained about it or thought it uncivilized. If you were caught doing something wrong you expected to be punished and that was the end of the matter. Each school had its own system. At Dartford, for instance, the teachers were all armed with their own cane (like thin bendy walking sticks) which they kept concealed in the sleeves of their gowns. When the occasion arose, they would draw their cane like a sword, whereupon dead silence would fall upon the room and everyone would look as innocent as possible. Justice there was always administered to the seat of the pants in front of the class. The younger boys had to bend over the teacher's knee while the older ones had to make do with a chair. The general result was the same either way.

At Wallingford there was a different system. There the reckoning always took place on Thursday afternoons. Sins were recorded throughout the week and if they passed a certain number the subject's name was called from a list on judgment day by the vice-principal, who made his rounds of the classrooms. The headmaster's office was at the top of a flight of stairs and on Thursday afternoons there was always a line of boys slowly rising, step by step, toward justice. The nearer one came to the study, the more distinctly the sounds of retribution could be heard from behind the door. This, of course, added considerably to the agony of waiting one's turn. Afterwards, we would go down to the washrooms, drop our pants and compare the marks on our bottoms. The boy with the brightest stripes became a kind of celebrity for the week. I never actually won first prize but there were a couple of times when I came in a close second. The cane was reserved only for boys. The girls were either too good or too fragile to participate in the Thursday afternoon massacre.

Waterloo was evidently more liberal than the other schools because I never heard of a caning there. I believe Dr. Tarrant, the headmaster, was what they called in those days "a progressive", which meant he was in the vanguard of the modern permissive movement. I think it would have been better for everyone had corporal punishment been administered because discipline there was decidedly inferior to that at Dartford or Wallingford.

One day, just before the lesson began, I was sitting on the window ledge entertaining the class with a ukulele I had learned to play. I was singing one of George Formby's songs, about what a window cleaner sees when he's cleaning windows. In the middle of the song, the teacher stalked in, pointed dramatically to the door and shouted, "Day, go to the head!" I got down from the window ledge and began to put away my ukulele but he said "Take that thing with you!" So, with trepidation I made my way to Dr. Tarrant's office and knocked on the door with my ukulele under my arm. Having been summoned to enter, I then had to explain what I had been doing and why I had been sent to him. It would have been so much easier to bend over and take "six of the best" on my backside, but instead Dr. Tarrant simply said, "Play to me!" It was horrible standing in the office singing to the headmaster about the window cleaner, but under the circumstances I sang at the top of my voice in the hope of gaining approval. Whether or not I was approved is unknown, but somehow I survived and after a lecture of considerable length on the importance of being subject to the teacher's wise leadership, I was allowed to return to my class.

By this time I was growing older and was becoming more keenly aware of the toll in life and limb that the war was taking. Soon after arriving in Liverpool a small package arrived for me. It contained a wristwatch and a letter saying that a young man named Tom, who had been a regular visitor to our home in Harwell, had been killed and he had left his watch to me. I was speechless and looked upon the watch in awe. It was not an expensive watch but it had been Tom's. To wear a watch on my wrist that had once graced his was a privilege beyond words. I was now in my early teens and extremely impressionable. Imagine my dismay when, a few weeks later, I realized that the watch was no longer on my wrist. I had no idea how or where it had disappeared but I was heart-broken by the loss. To me it was almost as if Tom had died all over again and this time I had been a party to it. It was weeks before the sun shone again in my life. Even now, over sixty years later, the thought of the loss touches me deeply.

Toward the end of the war Audrey and Archie were married. Archie, his sister, Jean, and some friends traveled up to Liverpool by train. This in itself was a miracle because Archie hated to leave the farm for any reason at all. Suddenly our house became very full. The girls all slept in one bedroom and Archie shared mine. He and I decided that we would put the vacuum cleaner under the girls' bed, with its hose poked in at the bottom, between the sheets, and its motor reversed to "blow". Then, when they were all happily tucked in we would switch it on. We set things up and the suspense was unbearable. Archie complained that he was "full of laugh" but managed to contain himself until the hour struck. The plan went off beautifully. The noise and screams coming from next door were most gratifying. At seventeen I was a rather young Best Man but managed to pull it off. Among the guests were two of the New Zealand airmen we had known in Harwell. One had been shot down over Germany and had spent several years in a prison camp. Due to ill health, he had been released in a prisoner exchange before the war came to an end. Both he and the other airman present had been awarded the Distinguished Flying Cross for gallantry.

D-Day

On June 6th, 1944, we awoke to find the sky thick with aircraft. Wave after wave of planes followed one another across the sky, creating a continuous roar. Many aircraft were towing gliders full of soldiers, all heading for France. D-Day had dawned and the beaches of Normandy were being assailed. The gliders were towed to within striking distance of their target and then released to land where they could behind enemy lines. Sadly, they proved to be less successful than expected and many men lost their lives in crash landings. However, a greater number survived and fought bravely in that great battle. The churches were all open on D-Day and many people interrupted what they were doing and went in to pray for the men who were fighting for their lives just across the channel.

Throughout the war years, the nation was inspired and held together by Winston Churchill. His unbounded optimism and strength of purpose transferred itself to the people. He knew how to communicate with them and give them courage, even during the darkest times. The king and queen also inspired confidence, choosing to remain in London throughout the blitz, and visiting areas destroyed by the bombing immediately after the raids. Their own residence was hit and suffered considerable damage. They justly gained the loyalty and love of the nation. Of course, the entrance of the United States into the war at the end of 1941 provided a huge boost in national morale, and the arrival of American servicemen in England was generally greeted with enthusiasm. It is true that there was a certain amount of antagonism on the part of some English people. This was due in part to jealousy over the fine material of American uniforms compared with the much coarser English ones, plus the luxury goods enjoyed by US personnel that were unavailable to the British people. In addition, the national pride of US troops in England tended to cause some of them to boast a little, which irritated their English hosts. But by and large they were cordially received, and lasting friendships (not to mention marriages) were made.

As the years passed I became more involved in extra-curricular activities. I joined the Air Training Corps and played the drum in the Cadet band. I learned to disassemble machine guns and put them back together, became proficient in Morse code and learned to identify allied and enemy aircraft by their silhouettes. I even went up to Derbyshire for a camp on an airfield and got in some flying. All the time the Allies were pushing the enemy further and further back into Germany. On May 2nd, 1945, final victory in Europe was achieved. Sadly, President Roosevelt died just 26 days before victory was proclaimed. On September 2nd, after the first atomic bombs were dropped on Hiroshima and Nagasaki, Japan also capitulated. During the six and a half years of war a total of seventy-two million lives were lost, worldwide, plus an unknown number of injuries.

That same year I graduated from school. Throughout my growing up years I had nursed the desire to be a farmer. My parents were not excited about the idea, partly because they had a suspicion that I was merely nostalgic about my days on Rocksea Farm and partly because they could see no way I could ever raise enough cash to buy and equip a farm of my own. They were correct on both counts, of course, but if I was not logical, at least I was determined. Somewhat reluctantly my father made inquiries concerning farmers who took in students preparing for agricultural college. He made contact with several and singled out one who lived at Tredethick Farm near the town of Lostwithiel in south Cornwall. In the dim past, Lostwithiel had been the capital of Cornwall but now it was just a sleepy town of granite and slate, nestled in the gorgeous valley of the river Fowey.

Tredethick, Cornwall

One weekend my parents and I traveled down to Cornwall to meet my prospective host. He and his wife had a lovely home and were most gracious. Their name was Liddicoat. Mr. Liddicoat was what was known as a "gentlemen farmer" because most of the actual work on the farm was done by hired men. It was agreed that I should become their student, live in the big house and be taught the ins and outs of farming. Upon my graduation from school I took the "big step", left home for the first time and went to live at Tredethick with Mr. and Mrs. Liddicoat. The first evening I was there, I chopped some logs for their fire and was hit in the eye with a piece of flying wood. It was an unfortunate beginning and I had to be introduced to the men with a patch over one eye, like a modern-day pirate.

The farm occupied a sheltered fold in the hills above the town. Ancient beech trees lined the driveway and in season snowdrops and bluebells grew in profusion on either side. The house was built in the traditional Cornish style of stone, rather low, with a slate roof. Orchards surrounded it, providing a sea of blossom in the spring. Cowsheds and barns, also built of stone, clustered round a square yard across the drive from the house, while all around green fields rose and fell in gentle folds. From the hill above the house, the ground dropped steadily down to the heavily wooded banks of the river Fowey. It was an idyllic location and on many occasions I sat among the trees watching boats make their way lazily up and down the river below.

I enjoyed farm life and became proficient in all kinds of skills. Tredethick was better equipped than many of the farms round about and by the time I joined them they used tractors rather than horses. Work which once had taken weeks could now be accomplished in days. I received a thorough grounding in all things agricultural but not all my efforts worked out well. One day I was given the job of riding the seed drill as we sowed wheat into a freshly prepared field. My job was not only to keep the box from running out of seed, but to make sure accumulations of weeds and dirt were not allowed to choke the drill openings, thus preventing the seed from running freely.

It was a beautiful day, rather warm for the time of the year. I remember the sweet smell of fresh earth and the mob of hungry seagulls that followed us round and round the field. Their cries, combined with the steady roar of the tractor ahead must have caused me to doze because it was some time before I noticed that several of the tines on one side of the drill were choked. How long they had been like that I could not tell, but I could see that the seed on that side of the box had not moved for some time.

We stopped the tractor and unchoked the drill. There was no damage done, as far as I could see, but from then on I paid more attention to the job I was doing. I soon dismissed the incident from my mind -- for a while, at least. But the matter was not closed. There came a day when the seed began to show above the ground. At first a green haze appeared, barely noticeable to anyone who was not looking for it. But as time passed, the lines of young wheat stood out for all to see. It was then I discovered the matter was not closed because round and round the field were strips of bare soil where the seed had not been sown. My day-dreaming, which until this time had been known own only to me, was now public knowledge. Mr. Liddicoat knew it, my workmates knew it, the neighbors knew it, and there was nothing anyone could do to put things right. The field sloped gently towards the main road, as if holding itself up for all to see how Ashley Day had cheated it of seed many weeks before. It was a long time before I was allowed to forget my sins.

Tredethick supported a large milking herd, which was milked by hand twice each day. I adapted to the task and soon learned how to keep up with the experienced men. Seed-time and harvest came and went, sunshine and snow, lambing and calving. Each passing phase brought its own interest and I enjoyed the privilege of working in such beautiful surroundings. Mr. Liddicoat was somewhat eccentric but on the whole he was a good boss and I look back on those days with pleasure.

While I was living at Tredethick, Cornwall was hit by a freak snowstorm. The temporal climate on the South coast of the county made snow extremely rare, but on this occasion it fell very heavily. I was awakened in the early hours of the morning and told to get dressed because we had to go out to care for the sheep. Cattle tend to face the storm and stay where they are but sheep turn their backs and run before it. Consequently, they end up against the far hedge, where the snow drifts are the deepest. I shall always remember the enchanting scene that met us as we set out in search of the sheep. The wind had sculpted fantastic shapes in the deep snow, so that strange pillars, almost like people, rose from the hedges or bordered the gates. A full moon shone in a perfectly clear sky, illuminating the scene and giving it an unearthly sheen. Sure enough, we found the sheep where the snow was the deepest and dug them out. Had we not done so they would not have survived until morning. Next morning I pulled three churns of milk down to the distribution center on a hastily made sled.

The Liddicoats attended a big Methodist church in town and I naturally went along with them. Though the teaching there was very poor, it was at least a church and I soon made friends among the young people.

We enjoyed happy times together. There is a castle just along the valley from Lostwithiel, called Restormel castle. It was constructed by the Normans in about 1100 AD and rebuilt in the late 13th century. At the time when I was there the Ministry of Works had not yet taken it over and so it was still unrestored and unspoiled. Ivy hung in thick canopies from its battlements and the natural growth of shrubs and trees had encroached up the mound on which it was built. It stood as it had stood for centuries and provided an evocative and romantic destination for the summer afternoon walks the young people often took together.

In the valley below the castle stood Restormel Farm. This was not quite as ancient as the castle itself but dated back to about the sixteenth century. I accompanied the Liddicoats to dinner there once. We dined in a cavernous hall with a huge fireplace at one end. The vaulted ceiling disappeared into the shadows above us and the light reflected from the paneled walls. The table seemed dwarfed by the size of the room. At the end of the meal, when the children were sent to bed, they disappeared down a long, dark passage opening from a balcony at one end of the hall. They seemed to be unperturbed by the shadows but I remember thinking that many kids would have been scared to death.

Old houses certainly can be spooky. Soon after I left for Tredethick my father was promoted again and posted to Burfield, near Reading. Leaving Liverpool my parents initially rented an old furnished house in the Thames-side village of Pangbourne. It was a rather dark house, still lit by gas lamps and exuded a distinct air of melancholy. Taking a break from the farm, I traveled up to stay with them there for a few days. The first night, I retired to my bedroom and got ready for bed. I felt strangely uneasy but could not tell why. I told myself to not be foolish, turned off the gaslight and jumped into bed. Almost immediately I began to feel there was someone (or something) in the room with me. The room itself became intensely cold. I relit the gas and looked around but there was nothing there -- just the bed, a big wardrobe in the corner, a dressing chest and a chair by the window. I looked inside the wardrobe but it contained only a couple of garments, placed there by my mother. Scolding myself for being foolish, I turned out the gaslight again and jumped back into bed. Once again I became convinced that I was not alone. Something was there and it was not friendly! This time I lit the light and kept it burning for the remainder of the night. Sleep eluded me but at least while the light was on the visitor stayed away. I have no explanation of what happened that night. I saw nothing, heard nothing and touched nothing. But the presence was so real that to this day I am convinced it was not imaginary. I did not mention my experience to my parents. Apparently they sensed nothing unusual about the house. Perhaps the phenomenon was confined to the room in which I slept. As for me, I kept the light burning for the remaining nights I stayed in Pangbourne.

Lostwithiel Town Band

Unfortunately, while at Tredethick I became involved with activities down in the town. This eventually brought my agricultural career to an end. Lostwithiel had a good town band. It met for practice in the rooms above the town hall chambers. I had always loved brass band music and although I had never learned to play a brass instrument I determined to find out what chances I had of doing so. One evening I went up to the rooms and introduced myself to the bandmaster. He eyed me up and down and then told me to take a seat against the wall. He then called the band to order and prepared to play a Souza march. As the music began (very loud in such a small space) I was filled with an excitement and thrill that sent shivers to the tips of my toes. At the end of the evening they sent me home with a trumpet and explained how I was to blow it. I did my best to master it but my lips proved too thick to fit the small mouthpiece properly so they exchanged the trumpet for a tuba. That had a mouthpiece large enough to cover half my face. I loved my tuba and made rapid strides in learning to play it. Poor Mrs. Liddicoat must have hated the noises I made in my bedroom but she was very patient and never complained. Each week I would carry the heavy instrument down the steep hill to band practice and lug it back again afterwards. I remember once blowing it over the gate of the meadow where the bull lived. He didn't appreciate it at all.

The time came when the band was booked to play at the Fowey Regatta. There we would play on the quay and eventually lead the Cornish Floral

Dance through the ancient streets. We were excited at the prospect and looked forward to it. On the morning of the event, I brought my tuba down to the kitchen to give it a last shine in the sink. Mr. Liddicoat came in while I was there and announced he was unexpectedly going to carry hay that day. I explained I was committed to the band for the regatta and he retorted, "Either stay and carry my hay or get out!" The challenge was too much for my rash temperament and I replied, "OK, I'll go!" With those "wise" words I walked out of Tredethick and carried my tuba down to the town, where the band was beginning to assemble. Looking back, Mr. Liddicoat had every right to expect me to cancel my engagement and carry hay. After all, that is why I was there and the unpredictability of the weather sometimes made snap decisions necessary. I was too immature to reason that out. Driven by my emotions rather than by reason, I reacted badly, all the while imagining that I was perfectly justified in my decision.

We had a great regatta but when it was over I realized I had nowhere to go. Had it not been for the kindness of some friends, who took me in for the night, I would have had to sleep on the street. I determined to visit Audrey and Arch in the hope that they would take me in. The next day was Sunday and the trains did not run all the way to my desired destination. I therefore rode as far as I could and walked the rest of the way. It was a very long walk to Audrey and Archie's farm but eventually I made it and they were given the doubtful pleasure of my unexpected arrival!

There were horrible rumbles when the news of my departure got back to my parents. Letters passed to and fro between my father and Mr. Liddicoat, ensuring that Mr. Liddicoat's version of what had happened was accepted as fact. Mrs. Liddicoat collected my belongings and mailed them home, which effectively brought my agricultural student days to a close.

By this time, my parents had bought a house called "Russets" in the village of Finchampstead. It was a beautiful location, with National Trust woods on one side, while in front fields swept down to the Hampshire border. I was now nineteen years of age and eligible for conscription into the forces. During my time on the farm I had been exempt from military service but now I had no cover. Consequently, I soon received a letter from the War Office, telling me to report to Brock Barracks, in Reading.

Military Service

In November, 1947, when the appointed day arrived, I duly presented myself at the barracks and was inducted into the army. Everybody knows what boot camp is like, so I won't go into the details. Needless to say, my buddies and I found it less than enjoyable and we were all glad when it came to an end. In my interview afterwards, the officer proposed placing me in the Royal Artillery to train for fire control (guiding guns to their targets). Foolishly, I objected that I was not good at math and he responded by putting me in the Royal Army Service Corps instead. It was entirely my own fault but too late to change. I was posted to Yoevil, in Somerset and began my service as a driving instructor. In this capacity I risked my neck daily, teaching recruits to drive trucks. Later, through the instrumentality of a friend, I was able to transfer into the pay office, where I served for the remainder of my time.

Life in the army seemed calculated to make one appreciate home. The hard reality of impersonal discipline made even the roughest soldier wish he were somewhere else. My solace was supplied by the local Methodist church, where the warmth and love of real people who lived in real homes ministered to me greatly. Not that I was strengthened in my theology while I was there. The young pastor doubled as a chaplain at the camp and he was extremely liberal in his theology. He told us that there was no such place as hell. He said hell was in our mind and we suffered, here and now, according to our manner of living. We were quite relieved to hear this because we were all a little uneasy about how we were living and it was comforting to be told that God did not mean what He clearly said in His Word!

Initially, National Service was for a period of 18 months. However, a few weeks before I was due to be released from the service, an additional six months were added. It was therefore not until November, 1949, that my military service came to an end and I was released back into the world. Now I had to decide what to do with my life. During my time at Tredethick I had been very impressed with a man named Wilfred Jeffery. He was mayor of the town and the organist in our church. Apart from those duties, he was also an auctioneer and estate agent. Many times I saw him in action in the cattle market and was struck by his eloquence and leadership capabilities. The result was that upon discharge from the army I no longer wanted to be a farmer but rather fancied becoming an auctioneer and estate agent. I therefore applied to a firm of estate agents in the neighboring town and was accepted as a trainee. I was disappointed to learn that they did not auction livestock but money was short and any job was better than none.

The parents of one of the secretaries in the office owned a television. These were still rare at that time and I had never seen one. The secretary invited me home one evening to watch this new attraction. There were no programs during the day. The screen merely displayed a geometric pattern until about six o'clock, when the evening's programming began. Then, of course, there was only one channel. The lights in the room were switched off and we sat around the television expectantly, watching the tiny nine-inch screen, which glowed a misty grey in the darkness of the room. At the appointed time music played and a shadowy image of a man appeared. I don't remember what the evening's programs were but I do remember I was greatly impressed. My eyes felt strained as I left the house, having stared at the little square of light in the darkness of the room all evening.

It was at this point that my single days drew to a close. I had claimed it was not my intention to marry until much later in life but this was actually a smokescreen. The truth was that I had a poor image of myself and found it difficult to believe any girl would marry me until she was desperate. Apart from that, I had not yet met one with whom I wanted to spend the rest of my life. I enjoyed the company of girls and had had a passing interest in one or two but none who really touched my heart. Love, however, has a habit of changing one's plans arbitrarily. It does not ask permission, nor does it give fair warning. It sneaks up unexpectedly and strikes, rendering its victim powerless to resist!

CHAPTER 2

Edna's Story

Shinfield, Berkshire

I was born on November 14th, 1929, the fourth daughter but fifth child of Herbert and Louise Kersley. My first vague memory is of being pushed by my mother in my high black pram (baby buggy). We were going down a long hill with beautiful old trees overhanging the pathway. The large houses on our left, bordered by broad green lawns, stood back from the road. As we neared the city of Reading they were replaced by smaller cottages, one of which was our destination, the home of my grandmother. She was a sweet little lady, a lot like my mother, but now with white hair and tiny gold spectacles. The home in which Grandma lived was very small. A fire burned in the black polished fireplace and a pretty teapot of purple, gold and red enamel sat on the hob in front of the fire, to keep warm ready for visitors.

My next vivid memory was one of being held in my father's arms wrapped in a checked wool blanket that felt rough to my skin. According to my siblings I had been very ill with pneumonia and not expected to live. "But God. . .!" Even then God had a much bigger plan for my life.

Why, I wonder, do we hold in our minds those cameo memories of certain moments in time? Is it because the happenings were rare, or maybe because the sun shone extra brightly to illuminate the colors around us? One such cameo, held so clearly in my mind, happened over seventy years ago. My mother was sitting on a park bench, surrounded by the greenest Spring grass and majestic old trees. In her hands, and spilling on to her lap, was a little child's dress of the most beautiful peach georgette. She was carefully picking it apart because we had all grown out of it. Lying on the seat beside her were two tiny dolls who were about to become the new owners of this much-coveted party dress, the skirt of which was composed of little frills, layer upon layer.

As mother quietly worked, my sister and I expended our energy rolling down a steep hill in the park and trudging back up again, checking now and again on the progress being made on the dresses. Much too soon the project was completed and after a little picnic in the park we headed for home, our dolls quite the prettiest they had ever looked, with their soft peach party dresses trimmed with tiny pink rosebuds.

I think, as I look back, that the memory is there because we so rarely had mother to ourselves. How precious each moment of leisure must have been for her then! She was the mother of five children, doing all the house cleaning herself and washing our clothes by hand (No washing machines were available in England for the masses until long after World War 2). I am so grateful for the example of unconditional love and humility she displayed before us. She truly had a servant's heart. Despite her workload, she still took time to teach us Christian graces -- to be kind and gentle to each other and anyone else with whom we came into contact and to pray each night before we went to sleep.

The house where I was born was quite small but fortunately it backed on to a large park where we children had plenty of room to play. A narrow, but deep ravine divided the park into two areas. One day my elder sisters were supposed to be taking care of me. I was around three years old. The older girls were jumping to and fro across the ravine and began to dare me to follow them. The result was my first broken arm. I wonder who felt worst, they or me!

It was around this time that it became obvious that our house was too small for our growing family. A move was therefore necessary. Our next house was in the same area of Shinfield but with much larger rooms and garden. So many memories of our time in this house are prompted by important lessons learned and my developing consciousness of color. For instance, I was spending some time with my Dad in the garden (a rare treat). He was digging a shallow trench in which to grow runner beans and explained to me the need to include goodness in the mix of soil. I think I must have become bored, so I skipped through the fence that bordered on a crescent of larger houses. To my childish delight I found a beautiful, many colored ball. It was so big I could hardly hold it in my small hands. Hurrying back through the fence with great excitement I proudly showed the ball to my father. To my surprise, he looked stern and asked me who owned it. I explained I had found it in the gutter. Needless to say, he sent me back to return it to the place where I had found it. With many tears I learned that the saying "Finders Keepers" is not always true.

Another important lesson learned at that time was that disobedience almost always led to tears. I guess I had been told not to play with my elder sister's beautiful china doll, but she was so much more fun than mine. I had been giving her a ride in a large cardboard box (a make-believe pram) when she accidentally fell out. I shall always remember her pretty face smashed into small pieces lying on the floor, quite irreparable. I am not sure which brought the most tears -- the beauty destroyed or the punishment received!

During this time I had arrived at the age for enrolment into school. To begin with it seemed fun to go off each morning with my sister, Beryl, who was eighteen months older than I. However, it was not very long before I realized that school meant learning about things I didn't always understand, and that teachers seemed to delight in making me feel foolish. Once, while still in my first grade class my sister was brought in from her class to tell me how to spell a word. For a shy, sensitive child, this was not a good teaching method. Fortunately I would not be in that school much longer.

Woodley, Berkshire

Sadness came into the family at this time, through the death of my uncle, the husband of my mother's sister. Because Auntie Eva had two children and was unable to work, my father agreed to help her by taking over the mortgage of the brand new house into which she had recently moved. We were on the move again, this time to a much nicer location in a country area named Woodley. Our family suddenly grew by three (my aunt, a little girl named Marion and her older brother, Gordon).

These proved to be fun years. My brother, Ron (the eldest child of the family) and my sisters, Olive and Barbara, were all in their teens, so life was lively. The house in which we now lived had much larger rooms and many more windows. It was a bright, happy place. After the initial sadness, it seemed to be filled with music and laughter.

My new school was quite different from the previous one; not the new modern building like my old school had been but a small Church of England school attached to the parish church, dating back to 1854, during the reign of Queen Victoria. My classroom was heated by a large open coal fire, with a high fire screen to protect the children, and was divided down the center by heavy red curtains. Since two classes shared the room it could be very distracting at times. It was rather like being in a crowded room with the conversation behind you sounding so much more interesting than that of the group you were with. I remember clearly that the bathroom facilities were very primitive. There were four sinks made of zinc and a couple of small cups hanging on chains that we all shared. Needless to say, the number of students was quite small.

My next school was brand new, quite different from the Church School in every way. The building was equipped with all "mod cons" but the staff, with the exception of a couple of teachers, was much like that at my first school. They seemed to delight in demeaning their students. It was not the peaceful, happy place of my previous little Church of England school.

Our school holidays were so much more enjoyable in Woodley because of the lovely country around us. Just up the road from our home was an old Elizabethan manor house, while on the other side of the gravel path stood an ancient farm house, shadowed by an old walnut tree. On one particular day the tree gave us shade from the heat as we passed beneath it. There were four or five of us children, the younger ones trailing behind the others. Our path led through a beautiful wood where, in autumn, we gathered chestnuts to roast in the open fire at Christmas time. However, today our thoughts were far from Christmas. They were consumed by the idea of the clear stream that flowed between banks of fresh green ferns and grass. As we crossed the field and wandered along the hedgerow, the sound of bees, the scent of wild roses and honeysuckle hung heavy on the air. Just around the bend and we would have reached our haven from the heat. Oh! The coolness and calm of this beautiful place! Socks and sandals were off in a moment and 40 little toes wiggled in ecstasy as the cool water flowed over our feet. This memory is just one of many such days during those early growing-up years in the lovely countryside of England.

After a couple of years, my aunt decided it was time for her to make a change and find her own home. My father helped her and soon she was settled in a place more suitable for her and her growing children. Those early days of my childhood, prior to 1939, were mainly happy and uneventful.

War Declared

On September 3rd, 1939 we heard the announcement that England was at war with Germany. For a nine-year old girl, who had never experienced a book or film about war, the announcement did not make much of an impact. Yet the air of sadness could be felt in the room. A few mornings later, just as we were preparing for the day ahead, the first air raid warning sounded, a sound that would invade our lives hundreds of times during the next five years. Its awful wail would tear us away from cozy beds, keep us from important classes and totally disrupt our lives. Soon we were issued with gas masks, taught how to use them and instructed never to be without them.

Our family soon became scattered. My brother, Ron, joined the army and was captured by the Germans at Dunkirk. Olive, my eldest sister, became a Land Girl and my next sister, Barbara, joined the Fire Service. That left Beryl and me at home with Mum and Dad. Some weekends were very special as my sisters returned home with all kinds of stories about their new lives.

Thoughts of God

As the days passed into years and we received news of my brother's capture, my mind often turned to thoughts of death. What would happen to me if I should die? I had been taken to Sunday school when I was younger but now, due to the war, we stayed close to home and the church was a bus ride away! I knew there was a God. I prayed to Him every night. But who was this person, Jesus? Were there two Gods? Had I been good enough to get to Heaven? As I lay in the darkness, with the drone of aircraft passing overhead, I tried to reason this out. I figured if my good deeds outweighed my bad deeds I might make it. If not, I felt sure I would find some friends in the other place, yet I knew I was a lot nicer than some of them! How ignorant I was!

I attempted to find answers to my questions by going to a small chapel in the village, but when I arrived a lady was replacing the pastor, who had gone to war. She handed me a King James Bible and asked me to read to the younger children. I did not learn much there and did not return.

Rationing

The war years were hard in many ways. Our daily lives seemed to be affected a great deal by the shortages. Due to the fact that we were living on an island, so much of our food was imported and the seas round about were infested with German U boats. Ration books were given to every person and strictly used.

The ration for an adult for one week was as follows: 1 Egg, 2 oz Jam, 8 oz Meat, 4 oz Bacon, 2 oz Tea, 2 oz Butter, 2 oz Lard, 2 oz Margarine, 3 pints Milk, 3 oz Sugar, 1-2 oz Cheese. Children were allowed one half of the adult ration. These amounts might not seem too bad on paper, but it was very difficult for a housewife to feed her family. Imported fruits, such as bananas and oranges disappeared for the duration of the war.

Farmers were forbidden to make cream from their milk and consequently ice cream was also unobtainable. Each person registered with their local shops and was provided with a ration book containing coupons. The shopkeeper was then issued with enough food for his or her registered customers. Each time a purchase of food was made, coupons were cut from the ration book to ensure quotas were strictly enforced. Stiff sentences were mandated for anyone found circumventing the law.

I think the shortage of coal for fires had the greatest impact on my daily life. Being a small, skinny child, except for hot summer days I seemed to spend those years perpetually cold. Each room of our house had a fireplace but because of the fuel shortage my mother would save the coal until the evenings when family members were all home. One of my most vivid memories of my dear mother was to do with her effort to keep us warm during a spell of very cold weather. I came home from school one day and found her in the coal shed with a shovel in her hand. She wore a bandana over her head and an old woolen coat pulled around her to keep out the cold. She was bent over sieving the coal dust in the bottom of the bin to save the small knobs of coal usually thrown away. Her main concern was for the welfare of her family. Little did she know that a number of times in later years she would be presented to King George V1, and later to her majesty Queen Elizabeth. Such was the life of the adult population. Much of their time was spent coping with extreme shortages.

Despite my mother's great efforts she was unable to keep the house warm enough to prevent frozen pipes. On one occasion when the thaw came, floods of water were pouring through the ceiling when we came home from school. Most of the time we children were sheltered from such difficulties and life was generally happy.

I can vividly remember the last time for many years that we were able to buy bananas. Our produce was purchased from a green grocer who came round each Saturday with a horse and cart. During the week he cared for his animals and land. One of his fields met our garden so we children would walk across the field and shop from his large barn. On this particular occasion, as my sister, Beryl, and I were crossing the field a plane came into view. This was not unusual because we lived close to a training airfield. However, as the aircraft drew closer we realized that its markings were very different from those on British planes.

We soon arrived at the farm house and knocked on the door, but as we turned to leave with the farmer, his son said, "Look, Daddy, that plane is dropping sausages!" It was actually bombing the airfield and some small cottages nearby. Fortunately nobody was killed but it was a scary experience.

There were other incidents that reminded us how precarious our lives were. One night we were again dragged from our beds by the air raid warning. There seemed to be more going on than usual. My father, who was part of the Home Guard unit, came home to report that incendiary bombs had been dropped in a wooded area about two miles from our house. The fires were soon extinguished. Of course, with the windows completely blacked out we were unable to witness the fire. Even the fire engines had just enough of their headlights exposed to see where they were driving (no flashing lights like we see today).

Close Call

The other really close call we experienced in our village was an attack by a lone aircraft one Sunday morning. It was quite early but light enough to see clearly. The milkman was busy delivering the milk when suddenly the peace and security were shattered by the close sound of machine gun fire. The pilot had brought his plane so low that we could see him from our bedroom window. He was firing at the milkman below but fortunately he was a bad shot.

Thus our days passed. Even though we may have been awake part of the night, school went on as usual. Maybe that (plus the fact that many of our teachers were elderly because the younger ones were away fighting) is why I was such a rotten student. We occasionally received cards through the Red Cross to say that my brother was alive. Sometimes they said he had been moved. Once in a while a very stilted (censored) note came from Ron himself.

My brother eventually came home shortly before the war ended, through a prisoner exchange program for boys who were ill. Ron was suffering from epileptic seizures, due to shell shock. He later developed TB and died at the age of about thirty. Only now that I have my own precious children do I fully understand the pain my parents must have suffered, knowing the terrible conditions my brother was living in throughout the war years. Later, to have him home only to die of the effects of his imprisonment must have been heartbreaking.

Back to Normal

At last the war ended. The whole world seemed to be happy again. Those who had survived returned. The blackout curtains were removed, gas masks were no longer needed. Warmth and color came back into my life. There were no more thoughts of death. I shall always remember the first Spring following the war. The grass and hedges seemed to be greener now, the birdsong sweeter. The lilac blossomed in profusion. It was as if the whole country had been reborn. However, another four years would pass before I received the answer to my question - "Who is this person, Jesus?"

Despite happy times, I also suffered some disappointments during those years. I realize, as I look back, that God was preparing me for salvation. After being badly let down by someone I trusted, I decided to get out of town on weekends. A friend, Jean, one of my work mates, introduced me to a group of young people in a cycling club. We would ride at weekends and on bank holidays. Cycling became an important part of my life.

However, one weekend I was unable to ride with my club because of work commitments. A friend came by and invited me to join her, her husband and an office friend, to ride to the coast the next weekend. Since I was free, I agreed. Ashley (the office friend) and I were introduced and after a couple of brief meetings we arranged to meet by the town hall in Wokingham fairly early on Saturday morning, August 1st, 1950.

CHAPTER 3

The Early Years

Trip to Arundel

The morning of Saturday, August 1st, 1950, dawned bright and clear. The sky was a deep blue and although it was still early in the morning the sun felt warm on our bare legs. The day promised to be perfect for a long ride. Edna and I met up in Wokingham and waited outside the town hall for our friends, Pam and Tony, to arrive. Edna was more of a "pro" rider than I, with more riding hours to her record and her bike supported her claims. Its name alone proclaimed its pedigree -- "*Sun Super Vitesse*"! It was light and racy and I felt somewhat clumsy in comparison. However, Edna pretended not to notice my inferior equipment and my initial apprehension soon subsided. After a while we saw Pam and Tony lumbering toward us riding "Bomber", their ancient black tandem, and within a few minutes we were ready to set out on our journey to Arundel. Arundel is a historic castle town in Sussex, about seventy miles from Wokingham.

As Edna put it, " It was as if God looked down and blessed that weekend from the outset. The sun shone, the bicycles performed well, we had no flats and the company was super. I found that my three companions had a wonderful sense of humor." Due to the fact that Pam and Tony both rode bomber, Edna and I spent all the time riding side by side. This turned out to be a pleasant experience and we chatted happily about many things as we went along. In those days, bicycles had very few gears, which meant that steep hills often had to be negotiated on foot. This added a new dimension to our journey as we trudged up many steep grades but it did nothing to dampen our enjoyment. Because it was a bank holiday the traffic was fairly heavy but nothing like the amount we see today. Roads were narrow, winding through beautiful scenery and often overshadowed by trees.

It was getting late when we arrived in the Arundel area and we needed to find somewhere to stay for the night. With great confidence we visited the local hostels and hotels seeking accommodation but they were all fully booked. We then approached several farmers in the area, asking if we might use their barns for the night but they all refused. We were thus left to our own devices. A grove of beech trees we had passed earlier offered good shelter so we retraced our steps and prepared to bed down there for the night. Our rain gear was pressed into service as a cover and decades of fallen leaves served as a bed. The night was mild and so, as we lay in a line together under our shelter, we were able to gain a night of fitful sleep. It was an interesting end to a very happy day.

Next morning we rose rather early, crumpled and unwashed but reasonably rested. Having made ourselves look as respectable as we could in the absence of water, we set off in search of breakfast. This refreshed us greatly and after a tour of Arundel castle and a visit to the beach at Worthing we headed back towards home. Due to our delays, evening fell before we had covered many miles. This time we were able to secure lodging at a private home that offered bed and breakfast. The house was situated on the edge of the village green and on the green itself was a fair. It was a small fair but there was something enchanting about it. The huge mechanical rides offered today were missing but the atmosphere was intimate and festive. We mingled with the village folk and shared their lightheartedness. Edna and I rode on a swing boat that was worked by pulling a rope. It was then that the sneaky feelings I mentioned earlier began to reveal themselves. It was fun, we were young and free, Edna was pretty and I was beginning to fall.

Full accommodation was not available for us all back at the house. The girls were given a bedroom but Tony and I had to sleep in the attic on temporary beds. The hot water pipes made strange noises during the night but we were too tired to let them keep us awake. Just before we went to bed, Tony and I looked out of our window that opened onto the garden. There on the lawn was a square patch of light shining from the girls' window below us and framed within it were their shadows, like silhouettes. We waved to the shadows and miraculously they waved back. Our own shadows must also have been visible to them. For some reason unknown to me, that insignificant episode intensified my feelings and I went to sleep that night thinking of swing boats, and Edna in the room below.

The luxury of a much needed wash next morning was greatly appreciated and after breakfast we set out refreshed. The journey home seemed to pass too quickly. The sun shone, the wind was behind us and the miles seemed to skip by as if they were eager to come to an end. Upon approaching Wokingham, Pam and Tony parted from us, heading away on Bomber toward their home. As Edna and I continued on together, conversation was not quite as free as it had been. It is surprising how one can chatter endlessly about things that don't matter, yet be tongue-tied when really important matters need to be discussed. I didn't want Edna to ride out of my life but I was not sure how to prevent her from doing so. I knew I should say something but what to say or when to say it escaped me.

Suppose she didn't want to perpetuate our friendship? Suppose she had some other fellow back in Woodley, or was too busy touring with her club? Suppose it was too soon in our relationship to raise the issue? I rode beside Edna trying to appear normal but feeling very abnormal inside. Eventually I found the courage to ask her if I could see her again and to my surprise she seemed reasonably favorable to the idea. I then suggested that she accompany me to church one Sunday and she agreed. This was indeed a breakthrough, releasing the conversation to flow again as it had before!

Edna writes, "At the end of our homeward journey, Pam and Tony left for home and Ashley asked if I would like to go to church with him. I had been pondering all weekend what made him so different from others I had met. He was so kind and gentle. Suddenly I realized that

I had met the first unselfish man in my life -- the first Christian man! Yes, I would like to go to church with him!"

After leaving Edna, I rode home, very excited. My parents were immediately subjected to a detailed account of our trip, especially of this special girl who had agreed to come to church. They were receptive but not quite as excited as I, due to the fact that they had heard similar enthusiastic stories before, none of which had come to fruition. Consequently, they showed polite interest but secretly adopted a "wait and see" attitude. I suspect my mother had been terrified for some time by the fear that I would turn up one day with one of those modern girls, thick with makeup and advocating feminine domination.

The next week dragged by slowly. Edna was committed to a night ride with her club the next weekend but thought she could make it the following Sunday. I had never looked forward to going to church quite as eagerly as I did during those days. Questions kept turning in my mind. Would she turn up? When she said "yes", had she meant "yes" or just "maybe"? Doubts lingered but when Sunday finally dawned I went to meet her. The bus arrived and sure enough, she was there. She really had meant "yes"! We were not yet completely "out of the wood", however, because Edna explained that there was someone to whom she had to talk before committing herself to me. Danger loomed and the next few days were filled with apprehension. But I need not have worried. All was well and our courtship was free to begin.

Edna writes: "After some weeks Ashley asked the question. 'How do you like my friends?' My answer was that I liked them but I did not fit with them. He kindly explained that they were Christians and that I could have what they had. He suggested that I go home and read John chapter 3. As I sat on my bed that night, reading from the tiny Bible my mother had loaned me, God's Holy Spirit revealed to me the answer to the question I had been asking for so long. I gladly asked the Lord Jesus for His forgiveness and invited Him into my life. Now I fitted! I was baptized and engaged to be married in the same month -- November 1950 -- on my twenty-first birthday."

Courtship and Marriage

Our courtship was not the kind of which fairy tales are made, except for the pure magic of being together. We had very little money and our time together was mainly spent taking long walks in the countryside. We often left Russets and walked up through the woods to what was called "the Ridges". This was a high ridge of ground from which a panoramic view of the Hampshire countryside could be seen. The woods themselves were beautiful. Giant rhododendron bushes had pushed their way upward in their search for light, and in the late Spring their exotic blooms of deep red, white with brown spots, pink and purple, hung in clusters in the soft light high above our heads. Ancient beeches, oaks and sycamore trees formed a canopy overhead while beneath our feet a thick carpet of leaf mold, formed during hundreds of bygone Autumns, cushioned our steps. I remember there was a bench on the ridges above the woods. We used to sit there together, looking out at the distant view and discuss how many children we would like to have, where we would like to live and what style of furniture we preferred.

On special occasions we scraped together enough money to go to a movie. The 40s and 50s might be termed the "golden age" of movies. Cinemas then were palaces compared with those today, with sweeping staircases to the upper floor, which sometimes housed a restaurant. Girls with flashlights would conduct you to your seat and there were often lines of people outside, waiting to purchase tickets for the next showing. These queues sometimes extended around the block and people were occasionally turned away. There were usually two films on the program (the main one and a supporting feature) and always a newsreel, which brought the audience up to date with world events. During the interval a theater organ, ablaze with colored lights, would slowly rise from beneath the floor and the organist would entertain the audience, while girls selling chocolates and cigarettes plied the aisles.

We knew of a tiny restaurant in Reading where we could buy mushrooms or cheese on toast and a cup of tea. This eased the budget considerably and we would sometimes go there instead of taking in a movie. In addition, church had a good youth group, where we made many friends. However, our favorite haunt was the beautiful village of Sonning, which lay beside a wide stretch of the river Thames and was within walking distance of Edna's home. Its narrow, winding street, bordered on either side by ancient buildings, gave it an air of romantic mystery that lured us back repeatedly. We just liked being there and never tired of its mature beauty.

On one occasion while at Sonning, I decided to take Edna boating on the river. We rented one of the wooden punts that were tied up along the bank and set out on our expedition. A punt is a wide, flat-bottomed boat that is sometimes propelled by a long pole, dropped down to the river bed and pushed. We didn't use a pole, preferring to paddle with oars. All went well for some time. Edna sat on a cushioned seat at one end of the boat while I paddled at the other. The sky was blue, the sun shone. Brightly colored dragon-flies hovered over the water and we enjoyed what promised to be a romantic afternoon on the river.

However, on our way back we heard a tooting noise and round a bend came a steamer -- the kind used to take passengers on river trips. I had always heard that river lore dictated that you move to the right of an oncoming vessel, so I paddled to the right. The ship, on the other hand moved to her left, facing us head on. When I saw what it was doing I paddled furiously to the left but the ship followed suit, all the time drawing closer and appearing much larger as the minutes ticked by. This happened two or three times, sort of in slow motion. In the end I figured that if it was going to hit us, the safest way would be to make contact head on, to avoid being tipped into the water. The ship kept making "ting-ting" noises as it drew closer and the passengers all rushed to the front to watch us drown. Luckily the impact was not violent since the ship, by this time, had reversed its engines. However it was enough to make Edna's end of the boat duck under the water, which didn't please her particularly.

Having finally disengaged our boat and pushed it round the side of the pleasure steamer, we made our way back to the place where we had hired it and were relieved to discover that the owner had gone home. This did nothing to change the fact that Edna had a wet bottom and I had definitely lost my seamanship status in her eyes. As usual, she was very understanding and endeavored to make me believe that the fault lay entirely with the steamship. I was grateful for her graciousness, but deep inside I had a sneaking suspicion that my handling of the boat must have had a lot to do with what had happened. We never went boating again, preferring to sit on the grass beside the river and watch the swans.

So our courtship progressed -- country lanes, woodlands, Sonning, mushrooms-on-toast at the teashop in Reading, the occasional movie and church -- nothing earth-stopping but beautiful to us. We soon learned that companionship is more valuable than the commercial pleasures that money can buy. During these times we talked for hours, drawing up our wedding plans and dreaming of our future together. To us, it was all very exciting. We were formally engaged one evening in Sonning, on a little bridge that spans the Thames. It was Edna's twenty-first birthday and a very romantic moment. Friends were scheduled to visit Edna's home to celebrate her birthday but I dragged her off to Sonning first for the "special event". Miraculously we made it back to Woodley in time to greet her guests.

Edna adds: "To me, our courtship was a very special and romantic time. We had so much to talk about, so much to learn about each other. I was learning how different it was to be loved and love unconditionally; to be in a Christian relationship where I was so happy to just be with Ashley. It didn't matter that most of our time together was spent walking or cycling. We were now trying to save for our wedding. I was also growing in my faith, not only in the Lord but in other people also. I had been badly let down by a number of people, especially by the young man to whom I had been engaged the year before meeting Ashley. Around that time I had observed marriages where the couples seemed cool and indifferent to one another, or where the husbands were so overly involved with their work and outside activities that their wives were left to raise the children alone. This was not the kind of marriage I wanted. I wanted a true companion, someone who would be there for me for a lifetime. I felt that in our relationship I had found the fulfillment of my desire."

Our wedding was planned for June 28th, 1952. The Lord blessed us with a beautiful hot summer day. Everything went according to plan. In English culture, weddings are planned differently from those in the States. The bride and bridesmaids traditionally dress at the bride's home and are taken to the church in hired limousines, which have white ribbons stretched from the front of the hood to the top sides of the windshield. People along the way see the ribbons and try to catch a glimpse of the bride. The bridesmaids go ahead in the first car and wait at the church for the bride to follow. When the ceremony begins, the bride enters first on the arm of her father and the bridesmaids follow behind as ladies in waiting, helping with the train and generally looking out for the bride's welfare. When we were married, Edna and her father, having driven about ten miles from her home in Woodley, arrived early and took refuge in the shade of some big trees until it was time for the wedding. It was supposed to bring bad luck if the bride arrived too early. As she drew up at the church, the sight of her three little bridesmaids and pageboy standing in the bright sun dressed all in white made a lasting impression upon her. Meanwhile, inside the church, the organist was playing a piece of music which contained a passage like the opening bars of "Here Comes the Bride". My Best Man and I stood up three times, thinking the bride had arrived, but then sat down again as the organ continued with the piece.

Milton Road Baptist Church was the venue for our wedding and Pastor Ray Smith was our minister. All went well, with the reception taking place in the rooms above the Rose Inn. However, in some ways the most satisfying moment of the whole day came when we had said goodbye to our families and guests and had taken off together in our little rented car, heading for the Cornish coast. We were married! As we hummed along the road to our honeymoon destination we felt free, cozy and secure. At last our dream had become reality and nobody could take it from us.

Honeymoon

Our plan was to stop in Axminster, Devon, for our first night. As we neared our destination we came to a place where the road dropped sharply and ended with a right angle bend at the bottom of the hill.

The road was narrow and high hedges rose on either side. As we descended the grade we were amazed to see an elephant, all alone, amble round the corner and make its way toward us. We had the distinct impression that it winked at us as it slowly passed us by. We discovered that it belonged to a circus and was being transported to its next engagement. The truck in which it traveled was not powerful enough to haul it up steep hills. It was therefore used to walking to the top under its own steam and waiting for the truck to catch it up.

We arrived at the hotel in Axminster too late for the evening meal but the staff graciously prepared a salad for us. Before entering the hotel we carefully removed all traces of confetti from our clothes, so that nobody would know we were newlyweds. Confidently we registered at the desk under our new title and a maid preceded us up the stairs to show us to our room. As she did so, she turned a couple of stairs above us and nonchalantly said, "By the way sir, you still have confetti in your hair!" Upon showing us our room she then remarked, "There are two beds, but of course, you won't need one of them, will you?" Then she disappeared from our lives, leaving her words to take up permanent residence in our memories. Despite our efforts, our secret was common knowledge and we felt a little conspicuous when we entered the dining room for breakfast next morning.

We had booked a cabin on the sands at Hayle, near St. Ives, for the week. We had found it advertised in the newspaper, where it was described in terms rather more favorable than reality revealed it to be. However, our lack of funds dictated that we be governed by price rather than luxury, so we had to accept the fact that we got what we paid for. The cabin proved to be one of those nondescript creations erected at that time on the dunes bordering many seaside beaches. Nevertheless, although it lacked aesthetic appeal it provided us with what we desired most, namely a nook where we could spend the next seven days in solitude. The bay was beautiful and we spent happy hours walking on the dunes. St. Ives, just along the coast, always a haven for artists due to its good light and quaint character, provided further enjoyment as we explored its crooked streets and art galleries.

Basildon Park

Once home, the task of finding a place to live became first priority. In England, after the war, accommodation was very difficult to find. The amount of property destroyed during the bombing, together with the influx of young men and women returning from the forces, made apartments to rent extremely rare. Eventually we read in the newspaper that a place was available on the estate of Basildon Park, where the BBC later filmed part of Jane Austen's "Pride and Prejudice". We applied immediately and were interviewed by the owner's daughter, a young woman in her twenties. She explained that she had used the accommodation as an art studio but was now offering it as a dwelling to make herself some pocket money. It had originally been an apple shed, one half built of brick and the other of wood. It stood in an orchard enclosed by an 8-foot high brick wall. A door in the wall gave access to the orchard, while around the wall were lean-to green houses, which once supplied out-of-season produce to the big house. It was a most unusual and romantic proposition. We agreed to take it without hesitation and a few days later we moved our few pieces of furniture into our new home. Edna's father helped us move and was obviously not impressed by what he saw. However, we were happy to be independent, despite the humble character of our abode. The atmosphere of the park was enchanting. Autumn was approaching fast and mists often hung among the trees, creating a mysterious atmosphere that summoned up pictures of bygone days, when the great house was vibrant with visitors coming and going in their carriages. To this day we refer to misty mornings as "Basildon mornings".

Unfortunately, Idyllic settings don't always guarantee comfortable living. Arrangements within our new home were somewhat basic. Cooking was done on an old kerosene cooker which had a very temperamental nature. Every now and then it would backfire and produce horrible smoke that clung to the walls and made everything smell. In the connecting area between the brick and wooden portions of the building a chemical closet had been installed. That was our only convenience. All other toiletries had to be done in the kitchen. In addition, the chemical closet had to be emptied and recharged periodically. This necessitated the digging of a deep hole in the orchard, into which the waste material was deposited. To make matters worse, we were sometimes awakened at night by a rat that seemed determined to gain entrance into our house. He would gnaw at the floor under the kitchen sink and at one point actually made a small hole. I filled the hole with a scrubbing brush and he promptly chewed it! When that didn't work, I stole from bed one night while he was gnawing and made a terrible noise above the place where the chewing was taking place. That stopped him for a while but soon he was back again. He never gained access to the house but he had a good try!

Basildon Park was situated near the village of Pangbourne, the beautiful village alongside the River Thames, where my parents had rented the "haunted" house. Edna and I would catch the bus outside the park gates each morning and ride into Reading. There, Edna had a Christmas job in the toy section of a departmental store and I went to work in the office of a real estate company.

We have happy memories of our short stay in Basildon but circumstances beyond our control brought our sojourn there to a close. One day I came home from work and found that Edna had made a brave attempt to dig a hole in which to empty the commode. She did not have the strength to go down very far so had dug a long trench instead. Consequently, the result was far from perfect and she discovered her tummy to be decidedly upset. Other smells began to affect her also and it was not long before it became apparent that there was a little one on the way. Wood Cottage was no place for an expectant mother and so we reluctantly gave the owner notice and moved in with my Mum and Dad at Russetts. We said nothing about our expectations but my mother recognized the symptoms during the Christmas holiday, when she noticed that Edna wanted to eat only celery.

Eventually, my job at the real estate company came to an end and I began to look for other employment. I applied for several and eventually received a summons from one of them to come for an interview. This was exciting because it came from a school of languages, situated in the center of London. I had been to London once or twice as a child with my father. He had shown me various famous places, such as

Buckingham Palace, Trafalgar Square, Westminster Abbey and the Houses of Parliament. On one occasion we had seen the king, queen and the two princesses. But I had always been awed by London's size and importance. The thought of actually going there to work each day was formidable.

School of Languages

When the appointed day arrived a friend insisted on driving us in her car. The journey proved to be somewhat chaotic but we made it up to London and located the school at the top end of Oxford Street. It was with some anxiety that I climbed the stairs to the office and was ushered into the presence of the CEO, Mr. Julius Schwarz. Mr. Schwartz came originally from Czechoslovakia and spoke with a strong foreign accent. He was a handsome, slightly built man of about fifty-five, with piercing grey eyes and an intense manner. When he was upset a vein became prominent in his forehead. A mop of grizzled gray hair framed his lean, tanned face and an engaging smile which revealed a row of even white teeth would suddenly dispel his otherwise rather fearsome appearance.

There were two schools. One taught foreign languages to English students and the other taught English to foreign students. In all, approximately six thousand students passed through its doors each year. The post for which I had applied involved record keeping for the School of English. In those days, before the advent of computers, all records were kept by hand, a daunting task with so many students coming and going.

The interview over, I was told to go home and await the outcome. The ensuing days seemed to drag but eventually a telegram arrived from the school asking me to go for a second interview. This time I was told that the list of candidates had been reduced to two, of which I was one. I returned home rather disappointed but found a telegram awaiting me to say that I had been selected for the job and inviting me to begin work the following Monday, 16th March, 1953. The salary would be £34.17.6 per month. That works out to roughly $67.86 per month at today's rate of exchange.

It was not easy to get to the school at the right time. The journey involved catching a train from Wokingham to take me the sixty miles to London, finding the right underground line to take me from Waterloo station to Oxford Circus and then walking up Oxford Street to my destination. The whole experience was new to me. I felt dwarfed by the huge buildings all around and overwhelmed by the crush of people, all of whom seemed to know exactly where they were going and how to get there. Somehow I made it on time the first morning. After that the commute grew more familiar and less stressful until, eventually, it became a normal everyday routine.

Life in the office was quite pleasant. I soon grew to know the staff and the many tutors who came and went throughout the day. At first, keeping track of the classes, the students in them and the tutors teaching them was overwhelming but as time went on the system became more manageable. We were all connected by a buzzer system on our telephones with which we could call other members of the staff, but Mr. Schwartz's buzzer was different. When he called, the buzzer continued until it was answered. It was all part of his technique to keep us on our toes. Sometimes we would be called into his office, which would strike panic into our hearts, but unless something really awful had happened, his extreme courtesy would soon soothe our shattered nerves, without ever diminishing our awe of him.

The office was situated quite close to Soho, a district renowned for its cosmopolitan character. Restaurants of all nationalities, and little stores that emitted strange odors, abounded. We enjoyed frequenting a little Greek restaurant that specialized in moussaka and rum babas. It had a Mediterranean smell about it and gave us a sense of being somewhere far away. There was also a little Italian store in Soho Square with strings of onions, garlic and bottles of Chianti hanging from the ceiling. It was necessary to duck when entering, to avoid becoming entwined. Soho was an interesting district in which to roam, though I understand it was not safe to do so after dark.

Our first daughter, Jennifer Lindsay, was born on August 17th, 1953. Edna had planned to have her at home but toxemia resulted in her being taken to Battle hospital, in Reading. This establishment was well named because of the brutal treatment Edna received there. She was admitted on August 14th and allowed to go home on 28th only after receiving a blood transfusion. This should have been administered much earlier. The nurses showed little sympathy for their patients' feelings. The doctors were also insensitive. In fact, judging by the treatment Edna received at their hands, "incompetent" would be a better description. However, despite a very hard time at Battle hospital, Edna eventually delivered a beautiful baby girl with whom we were thrilled. Once home, Edna slowly gained strength and was soon back to her old self. We were delighted to have our little girl. She added a bond between us that nothing else could provide. The staff at the office helped me celebrate by presenting us with a beautiful pink high chair which, with some difficulty, I managed to carry home on the train.

The daily commute from Wokingham to London being difficult, it was arranged that I should stay with my grandmother and aunt from Monday to Friday and travel home at weekends. My grandmother lived in Blackheath, a southeast suburb of London. The commute was therefore made considerably shorter. This arrangement, though easier for me was a hardship for Edna, who was left to care for the baby on her own most of the time. My mother was there but that was not the same as having her husband beside her to help.

Abbey Wood, Kent

In the Fall of 1953, we decided to look for a place of our own. There followed an exciting time, during which Edna and I visited homes in the greater London area in search of one we could buy. Eventually we found one in Abbey Wood, a community not far from the area where my mother and father had grown up. It was a sweet little bungalow, built of brick with a tiled roof and having three bedrooms, a large living room, kitchen and bathroom. It was the home we had been dreaming of. Mr. Schwartz took a keen interest in our search, introduced us to his own lawyer and even advanced us money to help with the down payment. On December 18th, 1953, we moved in and greatly appreciated the opportunity to live together again as a family. The railway station was just down the road and a direct line ran to Waterloo. From there I could walk to the office, so the daily commute was greatly simplified. Edna soon found friends in the neighborhood and on sunny afternoons they would take their babies to the park, or visit the "Well-Baby Clinic" together and enjoy times of fellowship.

Whenever you buy a house, you take a risk as to who your neighbors will be. We had one particular neighbor who unfortunately had an acute drinking problem. Each evening she visited the local pub and sometimes she would stagger home, quite late, very much the worse for wear. On these occasions she would embrace the lamp post at the corner of the street and treat us all to a recital of songs. The performance was excruciating and we would close all the doors and windows in an attempt to prevent her renderings from invading our house. Eventually she would wear herself out and roll away in the general direction of her home. Fortunately, she was alone in her habits. The rest of our neighbors were very respectable.

Life has a way of revolving and it happened to us. Abbey Wood was just a short distance from Erith, where my parents had spent their young days. For many years they had been active in the youth activities at Queen Street Baptist Church and now we also were able to attend services there. Many of the older folk remembered Mum and Dad and so it was rather like coming home. It was a good church and we enjoyed our time there.

One day a strange thing happened. It was a sunny Sunday afternoon and Sunday School was due to begin. As I approached the church I noticed an old lady resting on a low wall bordering the side walk. I did not know her but something about her caught my attention. She had a radiant face and seemed full of joy. She waited until I was level with her and then, with a sweet smile, she said, "Now here is a young man who will one day be a minister!" I was shocked by her statement. After all, I was securely established at the school and had never given the pastorate a thought. I never saw the lady again but the time would come when her words would prove prophetic.

In July 1955 Mr. Schwartz decided to create a new office for himself on the floor above the main room. Hitherto his sanctum had opened on to the main reception area. When the new room was complete he called me in and announced that I was to inherit his old office. This came as a shock, especially when he added that he was appointing me as the new administrator of the school of foreign languages, with an increase in salary to the equivalent of $84.83 per month. I moved into my new quarters with a feeling of awe. The walls were lined with polished mahogany paneling and Mr. Schwartz even left his big mahogany desk and chair for me to use. I felt strangely out of place as I seated myself behind the dreaded desk for the first time. I had been so many times on the other side of it that I felt as if I were trespassing on hallowed ground. Initially I sensed a kind of reserve from the rest of the staff but as time went by this eased. I suppose they became used to the fact that I had been given the good fortune of inheriting Julius Schwartz's sanctum and there was not a lot anyone could do about it. Time heals.

Another rather exciting event took place later that year. There was a flurry of excitement in the office when the Duke of Devonshire paid a visit to Mr. Schwartz. We knew the Duke didn't want to learn a language but had no idea what the meeting was all about. He was closeted with Mr. Schwartz for a long time and then later that month he came again. Something big was obviously being planned. Our curiosity was at last satisfied when the announcement was made that a property in Eastbourne belonging to the Duke had been purchased and was to be turned into a finishing school for young ladies. Our schools were to be closed for one day and the entire staff and their families were invited to travel down to Eastbourne, on the Sussex coast, to inspect Mr. Schwartz's acquisition.

With great excitement we caught the train on the appointed day and were taken to the property. It was an exquisite old mansion, standing in many acres of parkland and surrounded by gardens. The face of the building was covered with roses and made a picture quite suitable for a Jane Austen movie. Before showing us round, Mr. Schwartz made a short speech and told us that our daughters would be welcome to attend the school when they came of age. Romantic pictures formed in our minds of our children, dressed in Regency clothes, treading the grounds with parasols over their shoulders. The Eastbourne Ladies Finishing School was the main subject of conversation for many days after that.

On January 24th, 1956, our second daughter, Alyson Clare, was born. She came into the world at the British Hospital for Mothers and Babies, a Christian establishment far different from Battle Hospital, where Jenny had been born. The whole system was set up on a friendly, compassionate and efficient basis. There was even a small chapel where patients and doctors could go to pray. When a baby was due, a bell was rung and student nurses ran from every direction to observe or assist in the birth. The little cribs in which the babies were placed had wheels and at visiting hours the fathers had to collect them from the nursery and wheel them in to their mothers. As was true of all English hospitals in those days, patients were housed in wards rather than private rooms, so the sight of twenty fathers wheeling twenty cribs into the ward was quite spectacular.

CHAPTER 4

Call to Service

1956 proved to be a pivotal year. My office at the school was on the second floor, overlooking Oxford Street. Its windows were level with the upper decks of the many buses that passed. These buses carried advertisements of various kinds on their sides and since there was a bus stop right outside our building I had plenty of opportunity to observe them. In the summer of 1956 I began to notice a new advertisement that read "COME AND HEAR BILLY GRAHAM". My initial reaction was "Who is Billy Graham and who would wish to hear him?" But as time passed, and the advertisements passed my windows with insistent regularity, the nudge to attend a meeting became stronger. As I look back, the nudge obviously came from the Lord, though at the time I had no idea that He was involved. Edna and I discussed the matter one evening and decided to go to Harringay Arena to find out what all the fuss was about and hear what this man, Billy Graham, had to say.

It was raining when we arrived at the arena and we were informed that it was already full. However, an overflow meeting had been hastily arranged in the greyhound stadium next door and we dutifully took our seats there. We were distinctly suspicious but as the service began we had to agree that although it came through loudspeakers from the building next door, the singing of the choir was outstanding. George Beverly Shea sang "He's Got the Whole World in His Hand" and then Billy Graham started to speak. The rain continued to drizzle and it was cold in the outdoor stadium where we sat. The miserable conditions definitely quenched any emotional reaction but as Graham spoke it seemed that something happened deep down inside. I have no idea what he said that day but when the invitation was given both Edna and I knew we had to respond - not for salvation because we had both been Christians for some time, but we felt the call to serve the Lord. We went forward with the crowd and were immediately approached by counselors. Neither of us gained much from them but the conviction remained and we both knew a change of lifestyle was forthcoming.

Edna remembers it differently. She remembers that the message Billy Graham gave that day was the clearest she had ever heard on the need for men and women to be saved. We had been fed a weak Gospel message for so long. A real hell was never mentioned. Our problem now was that we had no idea how to proceed. It was one thing to say "yes" to a call but quite another to know how to follow it up. Unlike young people in the USA today, who have opportunities thrust upon them from all sides, we had no example to follow. We knew that most evangelical pastors within our sphere of knowledge had attended Spurgeon's college and so we assumed this would be the way to go. Even then we needed someone to advise us and give us competent guidance. We decided that the very best person to contact would be the president of the Baptist Union of Great Britain. I had been a Baptist all my life, and who could be better to guide me than the leader of my denomination? If he would not meet with me there would no doubt be someone else who would condescend to give me an interview.

I telephoned the union offices a day or two later and to my surprise the president agreed to see me. We made an appointment to meet next day in Lincoln's Inn Fields, the London square where the leading lawyers have their offices. At the time appointed I met the president and told him of my experience. As we walked around the square he listened carefully, asked me where I worked and how many children I had, what my prospects were, etc. Then he told me very forcefully that I would be irresponsible to leave my job and jeopardize the security of my family just to go to Bible college. I should forget it, settle down where I was and care for those who relied upon me! In doing so, he ignored the call I had undoubtedly received and disregarded the fact that God had spoken to me at the Harringay meeting. Nevertheless, he was the leader of all English Baptists. Who was I to question his wisdom or disregard his counsel? I went back to the office rather deflated and tried to forget my call. I didn't want to be irresponsible and I certainly didn't want to jeopardize the security of my family. But somehow the sparkle had disappeared from life. I was no longer settled and work seemed to have become dull and pointless.

If I should not go to Bible college, how else might I fulfill the call God had placed upon my heart? One evening after supper Edna and I discussed our alternatives at length. I remember Edna saying that she felt that if people were heading for hell, how could we be concerned with just our own family and not for the millions who were lost. As we look back we realize this thinking was the work of the Holy Spirit making our call real. Our house, which we had been so excited about just a few years earlier, now seemed to be an obstacle holding us back from serving the Lord. We were young, self-centered and not well taught. We can receive no praise for this at all. It was all by God's grace that He chose to call and lead us and we are deeply grateful.

My sister, Audrey, was (and still is) a lay preacher in Cornwall in the Methodist circuit and we felt that perhaps I might be allowed preach there. The difficulty would be in finding a way to earn a living in such a rural area. Jobs were few and far between. Then the old farming instincts presented themselves and we thought perhaps a small farm might be the way to go. With feelings rather like those of explorers planning an expedition we secured local newspapers and began to search for small farms to rent. They were scarce but we found two or three. I remember there was one in south Cornwall that looked promising but the rent was too high. Then my parents found one on the moors above Camelford. It included a house, outbuildings and sixteen acres of land. The rent was within reach and so we made contact with the owner. Negotiations were successful and we entered into a contract.

The next step was to place our house on the market for sale. This we did and very quickly someone agreed to buy. With the house sold all I needed to do was give notice at the school. Mr. Schwartz's new office was huge. It seemed like a hundred yards from the door to his desk. Having made the journey and sat down in the proffered chair I managed to tell him what we had done. He listened very graciously and then arose and asked me to accompany him. We left the office and crossed Oxford Street to a large building on the other side of the road. This, he said, was to be the new school. A great marble staircase curved up to the floor above, where our offices were to be located. He reminded me of the college in Eastbourne and told me I was even mentioned in his will. Did I still want to leave? The struggle was intense. To remain in London promised financial security and advancement. To leave meant heading out into an unknown future with no guarantee of support. But the call was still there and I knew I had to make the choice. I told him I felt I had to move on and he accepted my decision.

In later years we have spoken to many ministers and missionaries who had similar experiences. It is common for those who are about to give up secular work in order to serve the Lord to be offered some great opportunity provided they would change their mind and remain where they were. Maybe it is Satan seeking to undermine their resolve or perhaps it is the Lord testing them. Whichever it is, it helps to confirm the reality of the call because the decision carries a price.

Temporary Employment

The following weeks were spent preparing for our move. It seemed as if everything was working out according to plan but then came a hitch. About a week before my notice at the school expired the real estate agent contacted us and said that the buyer had pulled out of the sale. That posed a problem. We now had no job and no sale! Nobody could tell how long it would be before another buyer came along, so I was obliged to look for another source of income. It was just before Christmas and I had heard that they were hiring seasonal porters at Waterloo station, so I went along and applied for a job. The following Friday evening I left my beautiful mahogany office and on Monday morning I presented myself for work as a porter. The foreman took one look at me and decided I was not normal porter material. He gave me a porter's cap, took a bunch of keys down from a hook and assigned me to clean the rest rooms on platform three. Unfortunately, many of my ex-colleagues traveled from this platform and although mercifully I never ran into one I was constantly on edge in case I did. After the day's work, I would go home, hiding my porter's cap under my coat, and smelling strongly of disinfectant. No germs came near me during those days.

Apparently I passed the test because after a while I was allowed to work as a proper porter, helping passengers with their luggage and pocketing tips for my efforts. Some evenings I came home with a pocket full of change that I had earned in tips. Sometimes I had to work late, cleaning trains that remained in the station overnight, or moving mountains of mail bags to sorting areas. On one occasion I missed the last train home from Waterloo and had to walk to London Bridge station, which offered a later train. The way led through one of the rougher parts of London, where gangs haunted the streets. There was no traffic at that time of night and the streets were lonely and deserted. My own footsteps seemed to echo unnaturally as I walked. I held my breath as I approached a shadowy group of young men gathered under a street light. They stopped talking and eyed me as I passed and a prickly feeling ran up and down my spine. I tried to look confident and carefree but felt extremely vulnerable. Mercifully, nothing happened and I made it to London Bridge where I caught my train home.

The Move

After some time the house sold and we were free to make our move. We arranged for a removal company to take our effects down to Cornwall and set the date for our departure. There was one last thing to take care of -- we needed a car to transport the family. A couple of days prior to leaving Abbey Wood, I visited a car dealer to see what was available. Unlike America today, where used car lots occupy every street corner, in the England of 1956 cars were not very plentiful. I knew of no car lots but some garages had two or three vehicles for sale. Enquiries had to be made in order to find them. The dealer to whom I went had a small number of used cars within our price range but one in particular caught my eye. It was a Rover in very nice condition. The problem was its size. Gasoline was still strictly rationed and this one would certainly not be very economical. However, we had been so long without a car of any description that the temptation was too great. I surrendered to the lust of the eyes and purchased it. It was a very pleasant experience, looking down the Rover's long shiny hood as I drove it home.

We finished packing most of our things and then Edna took the children on ahead by train to her parents' house in Reading. I remained at the house over night to ensure that the movers did their job properly. Tired from packing, I overslept and they caught me next morning in bed. I awoke to the noise of banging and realized the movers were standing outside waiting to begin their work. They didn't seem to mind my condition but began to move furniture from other rooms while I made myself respectable. The work was finally completed and the men took off, leaving me to do a final clean and lock up.

It was getting dusk by the time I left the house and a thick fog had descended. Knowing the immediate area I was able to make my way out of Abbey Wood but then I was faced with driving across London, in a strange car, and finding the Reading road on the other side. I made it as far as Blackheath, an open area of common land with no landmarks to guide. The fog thickened and visibility was reduced to about three feet. The headlights merely accentuated the density of the wall of white ahead and I found myself disoriented. After a while a huge shape loomed up ahead which I recognized as a bus. I knew the London bus drivers were well acquainted with their routes, so I tucked in behind him and followed closely, believing he would at least lead me across the heath. However, before long he stopped and I realized he too was lost. There was no choice but to wait where we were in the hope that the fog would lift. It was a strange experience, rather like being packed in a box of white cotton wool, with no entrance and no exit. Nothing moved, except for the bus driver who passed the time talking to his passengers.

I don't know how long we waited out there on the heath, but eventually the fog began to lift. Gradually we were able to discern shapes as trees and sign posts became dimly visible. The bus started up and very slowly we inched our way across the heath to civilization. Once back in the city, the lights helped to dispel the fog a little and progress was speeded up. Miraculously I found the Reading road and arrived safely at my destination a couple of hours later.

Next morning the sky was clear and we set out on our journey to Cornwall. Due to gasoline rationing travel was still strictly limited. I had the coupons assigned to me but they were insufficient to take us all the way. My father came to the rescue by giving us his coupons and we calculated that with the two rations combined we had a fair chance of reaching our goal. However, we had not driven far before the fuel gauge indicated just how fast our gasoline was being used. We could almost see the needle moving toward "empty". The car was beautiful but it was becoming obvious why the previous owner had sold it. Equally clear was the fact that we could not afford to keep it very long ourselves. Service stations were widely spaced in those days and we carried gasoline in cans. Stops to pour in more fuel were startlingly frequent and we wondered if we could stretch our coupons sufficiently to complete our journey. It was comforting to reflect on the fact that we were in a car and not in an airplane!

After a suspenseful journey, we finally found ourselves on Bodmin Moor, just a few miles from our destination. There we stopped to empty our last can of gas into the tank and then made a run for home. It was with great relief that we drew in through the gates of Glenfields, where my parents now lived following Dad's retirement. The sense of security came as a great blessing after the tension of our journey. Jennifer, of course, now three years old, had no comprehension of our anxiety and looked upon the whole affair as an adventure. Alyson, at 11 months, could not care less and was simply pleased to get out of the car and experience some freedom at Grandma's house.

CHAPTER 4

Highertown, Cornwall

Next morning my father drove us over to our new home. It was known as "Hightown" in the parish of Advent. We had seen narrow roads over the years but nothing like those which led up the winding hill to Highertown. Hedges up to twenty feet high on either side made the way seem more like a tunnel than a road. Each bend brought a climax of fright lest a car should come round it in the opposite direction. There was no room for two cars to pass. If one was encountered, a quick calculation had to be made to decide which one had passed a gateway most recently. He had to back up and squeeze into the gateway while the other driver went on his way with a polite wave of the hand. That was life on the moor and over the next few years we would become quite at ease with it.

About a quarter mile from our house we emerged from between the high hedges and crossed a little stone bridge over a stream. A rocky track then turned sharply and made its way to the top of the hill. There we found, a small stone chapel, three cottages and a bright red phone box. The fields were separated by ancient stone walls covered deeply with moss and tough grass. A sweet smell of heather and sea air filled our lungs as we left the car and took our first look at what was to be our home for the next three years.

For a moment we stood outside viewing the house. It was a typical low Cornish cottage, built of local stone and having a slate roof. The front door, protected by a small porch, occupied the center of the building, with windows set in white frames on either side. Above them, matching windows indicated the position of the bedrooms. The outbuildings were attached to the end of the house, making a long continuous structure. On ground level there was a cows' house and a large separate stall, while upstairs was the corn loft, where grain and hay were stored. A stone-flagged walkway, about twelve feet in width, ran the length of the building and on the far side of it rose a natural stone wall, about eight feet high and approximately six feet thick at the base. Although this blocked the view and some light, it also sheltered the house from the prevailing winds that occasionally blew in from the Atlantic. There were no windows on the rear of the house but the long wall was broken by a set of stone steps that led up to the loft door above the cows house. Beyond the steps a large square structure stood out at right angles to the outbuilding. We later used this to house our chickens.

On the east side of the house, small fields swept down into a steep valley and on the far side, about a mile distant, rose the white hill (or "tip") of a china clay works. Every few minutes we would hear a distant clang as a trolley ("skip") full of white quartz sand was pulled to the top of the hill and emptied. Beyond the clay works, Bodmin moor stretched for miles, wild and lonely. Daphne DuMaurier made this area famous with her book, "Jamaica Inn". The ancient mystery of the moor has to be experienced to be appreciated. Long before the Romans came to conquer the land, primitive peoples roamed its rocky spaces and left behind monuments and burial places that are still there today. It is almost as if their unseen spirits continue to lay claim to the land.

Inside the house we were met with a scene we had only vaguely expected. The floors downstairs were paved with large squares of slate. Due to the age of the building, these had been worn into smooth uneven shapes by many generations of feet. The house had been unoccupied for a while, and therefore felt cold and slightly damp. The small recessed windows revealed the eighteen-inch thickness of the walls. A wooden wall separated the main room from a small kitchen and a little staircase led upstairs to two bedrooms. There was no bathroom, no running water and no sanitation -- other than the outhouse on the walkway outside. Occupying most of the west side of the room was a huge open fireplace, blackened with soot and glistening in places where rain had trickled down the chimney and run in tiny rivulets into the fireplace. I looked up the chimney and saw sky not very far above. The damp soot sent a bitter aroma throughout the house, giving it a desolate, forsaken air. Obviously a lot of work had to be done before the house was fit to move our little family in.

For the next month, Edna and I busied ourselves with the project. My parents lived close enough for us to leave the children with them while we took off each day to work on the house. A major issue was how to heat the house and cook our food. For the previous two hundred years, tenants had contented themselves with a peat fire in the fireplace but we drew the line at that. We agreed that we had to purchase a solid fuel stove and convert the fireplace into a recess to accommodate it. The first step was to build a wall across the width of the chimney breast, effectively cutting it in half and then to install a metal ceiling above through which the cooker's chimney could be sealed.

We ordered a stove and I purchased some concrete blocks with which to build the wall. With no experience of such things, I built too high too fast and in the morning my new wall had collapsed. I cleared away the mess and began again. This time I built half way and waited for the cement to set. Then I went the rest of the way. It was not too difficult to install the piece of sheet metal to seal the chimney. After a coat of white paint had been applied to the new wall and ceiling, the stove was brought in, its chimney poked through the hole prepared for it and we were in business! The whole room looked brighter and cozier once the old sooty fireplace had been covered up and a fire was burning in the stove. The house soon warmed up and we were able to sit down and figure out what to do next.

Mice posed another problem. Due to the fact that the outbuilding roof formed a continuous unit with that of the house, the mice thought the house was part of their domain. Somehow we had to convince them that this was not the case. We trapped and painted and cleaned for approximately a month. After our furniture arrived, the house seemed much more cheerful and we finally decided it was time to move in.

Although the primitive nature of our new lodging was very evident to us, Jennie was quite oblivious to it. She moved in happily and was soon outside exploring the fields and enjoying the fresh air and freedom. She thought it was great! Alyson was not yet old enough to care either way.

Life on the Moors

We were now living on a small acreage but had no livestock, no income and no means of support. I had to do something quickly. A sawmill down in the Allen valley, five or six miles away, was advertising for a truck driver. In view of my army training I felt I could manage their truck so I applied for the job. The owner looked at me doubtfully and scratched his chin, obviously wondering if I could meet his requirements, but eventually he agreed to take me on. Commuting to and from work meant riding my old bicycle down hill to the mill in the morning and then walking most of the way home when the day's work was done. I didn't even have a three speed gear so riding up the long hills was impossible.

Sawmills in the USA today are computerized, well-oiled machines. Mewton's sawmill was not. A co-worker and I were sent out to specific places to cut down specific trees with a crosscut saw. They were then limbed with axes and the logs rolled up two planks on to the truck using ropes, peavies and wedges. Once home, they were cut with a saw powered by an antiquated donkey engine. It took four or five of us to start it with a large crank. Once it was working, the logs were manhandled onto the bed and cut into useable lumber. It was a wonder nobody was killed. A team of men manufactured gates and chicken houses with the sawn lumber and I was sent out to deliver their creations to neighboring farmers.

I soon discovered why the boss had hesitated to hire me. I was an office worker and unused to hard manual labor. Sawing for hours with the crosscut and struggling with the heavy logs demanded more than I had to give and the long walk home at the end of the day, pushing my bike, left me exhausted. However, as time passed my muscles began to attune to the demand made upon them and eventually I was able to cope without any problem.

The neighboring farmer agreed to let us draw water from the faucet in his yard and for three years we carried it back to our house each day in buckets. We built a little counter in the room we called the kitchen, which apart from the name had no resemblance to a kitchen. We also set up a small table there on which we ate our meals. After a short while, we began to see life come to the holding. Archie gave us an old Guernsey milk cow named Fanny and a local farmer agreed to let us have some sheep in exchange for half the wool and half the lambs. In addition we added some chickens and geese to our menagerie. We were looked upon as "townies" by the local population but they were kind and often gave us advice, especially at lambing time when it was most needed.

Milking soon became a daily routine. It was a blessing to have plenty of fresh milk and Edna made good use of it. On cold mornings it was very relaxing to do the milking. The sweet smell of hay and the sound of Fanny happily chomping in her stall; the warm hollow in her flank that fitted one's head nicely and the frothy hiss of warm milk squirting into the bucket all combined to give a calming affect as the day began. Sometimes, of course, Fanny would swish her tail across my face, which was irritating, but generally speaking cow's house relationships were very good and we were grateful for Fanny's contribution to our lives.

Perhaps the most inspiring thing about this phase in our lives was Edna's uncomplaining attitude. She had come from a modern house, with modern facilities to a dump of a place with no water, no electricity and no sanitation. She had to cook on the solid fuel stove and care for two small children. Diapers had to be washed by hand and the kids had to be bathed in a tub by the fire. She did the washing by hand with the water we brought in and then carried it down to the bottom of one of our fields to rinse it in the stream. She hates mice and we had a plague of them when we first went to live at Highertown, yet not once did she complain. She accepted our primitive situation as the Lord's leading and determined to make the best of it. She was twenty-seven years old.

All kinds of crises made life on the moors exciting. When the weather was calm Highertown was the epitome of peace. The clear, sweet air was exhilarating. Herbs which grew only in that area added a distinctive aroma that was a joy to breathe. During the winter, when the night was clear and the moon was new, the sky was filled with millions of stars. No man-made lights were present to dim the display. From horizon to horizon the glory of God lit the heavens in the most awe-inspiring panorama of starlight. However, when a gale blew in from the Atlantic things changed dramatically. Trees bowed in the wind and gates rattled on their hinges. Any attempt to walk resulted in one staggering like a drunken man. It was on such a night that our outhouse blew over! The night was dark and the wind was blowing too hard to stand it up, so Edna and I had to work out an emergency system before retiring for the night. With some effort I managed to retrieve the pail from the outhouse and carry it into the cows house, where Fanny was placidly chewing hay. I then held the lantern for Edna and she held it for me. Fanny looked on unmoved and quietly contemplated the extraordinary behavior of humans.

Due to the gasoline rationing, it was obvious that our big Rover car would stand idle most of the time. It was beautiful to look at but was just not practical. We therefore decided to drive it into town and see if we could find anything more economical that we could swap for it. We soon discovered that nobody wanted to exchange anything worthwhile for it. Eventually we found a man who had an old green delivery van. He was willing to do business, so we made the exchange and drove away in this ramshackle vehicle that rumbled and rattled over every bump. Jenny sat on the floor in the back and laughed all the way home because she thought it such great fun to ride in such a noisy vehicle. It was long past its prime and was reluctant even start. However, it was all we had and we were obliged to make the best of it.

About a year after we moved into Highertown, I heard of a job being offered by a grocery store in the local town. They were looking for someone to take on their ice-cream van, which toured the area serving the outlying villages. My job involved driving into a village and ringing my bell. Hopefully, the local inhabitants would all run out to buy ice-cream. Sadly, most did not. It seemed to rain continually while I was employed there and the number of people wanting to buy ice-cream in that weather was small. Though it was a pleasant change from sawing logs, it was a lonely kind of job. Some days I drove many miles and sold very little. Not that that seemed to worry the boss but I felt jilted.

We were extremely poor during those days. I had managed to install some propane lighting in the living room but sometimes we could not afford to replace exhausted tanks and were obliged to revert to oil lamps and candles. The Christian owner of a hardware store in town was very kind to us and extended us credit to buy feed for the animals. Humanly speaking, without his help we might not have been able to make it, but that would have discounted the provision of the Lord. He always provided food for us to eat and clothes to keep us warm. 1 Timothy 6:8 says, "Having food and clothing, let us be therewith content", and we were. The children, of course, had no idea that we were so short of money. Life for them was free and fun, with an endless amount of room in which to play.

China Clay

My break came when a neighbor tipped me off that there was a vacancy at the clay works. Jobs there were coveted because the company was about the only business in the area that offered secure employment. I had not applied up to that point because I knew there were no vacancies. The manager (or "captain", as he was called) was sympathetic to my story, and since I came with the recommendation of some of his respected workers, he gave me the job.

China clay, or kaolin, is formed of decomposed granite and still retains the ingredients of granite (mica, quartz and feldspar). The clay is used in many ways. Cosmetics, toothpaste, motor tires and many other commodities contain kaolin. Strangely, the only part of actual chinaware in which china clay is used is in the glaze which is applied to the outside of china pieces. The clay works, or clay mine, consisted of a deep open pit, covering forty or fifty acres. The clay was washed out of the cliff by powerful hoses and ran down like milk to pumps which elevated the liquid to the surface. There it was dried in open beds, heated and taken away in the form of powder. The tiny quartz crystals released from the material accumulated in heaps of white sand on the floor of the pit and were scooped up by what was called the "scrape" - a big digger on cables. This filled the "skip", which was hauled up rails by cables to the top of the hill and dumped. Over a number of years, these "tips" grew very high and were familiar features of the landscape in many parts of Cornwall.

With the clay and the sand removed, seams of rock were left protruding out of the cliff like bones. These had to be removed and my first job was to break them with a chisel and sledge hammer and wheel them away in a wheel barrow over a series of wooden planks, to a place where the scrape could take them away. I had thought life at the sawmill was tough but it was easy compared with this. By the end of the day I was ready to drop! Mercifully, it did not last very long. After a while I was relieved of that task and promoted to one of the hoses. These were powerful canon-like hoses, mounted on wooden bases to keep them steady. It was chilly, damp work but much easier on my back. The company supplied oilskins to protect us from the constant spray when the wind blew in the wrong direction, enabling us to remain reasonably warm and dry.

Life on the hose could be boring but sometimes a wake-up call came un-expectedly. One day I was working the hose up a narrow gully. The sides of the pit towered above me on both sides and the stream of milky water rushed down the rocky slope beneath my feet. I noticed a small stone tumble down from above but took no notice of it. Then another bounced toward me and then some more. I looked up and it seemed as if the whole world were caving in upon me. It was almost as if the cliff was collapsing in slow motion, sort of suspended in mid-air. Without waiting any longer I took to my heels and ran as fast as I could. A huge crash behind me shook the ground and when I glanced back I saw a fifteen-foot wall of white mud and rock bearing down upon me. I kept running until I was safely out of the gully and into the main pit. It was a major cave-in and if it had not been for those small stones that alerted me to the problem I would have been buried beneath many tons of mud and irrevocably lost. It took us weeks to clear the debris and recover the hose.

Lay Preaching

About this time I was confirmed as a lay preacher and assigned churches in which to preach each Sunday. In the 1740s John and Charles Wesley had been busy in the area and a revival had broken out under their ministry. In the wake of the revival many small stone chapels had been built, which still stand today. Unfortunately, the spiritual fire grew dim over the years so that whereas the chapels were once filled to overflowing, now just a handful of faithful believers attend each Sunday. Almost every village has its chapel and it is in these that the local preachers hold their services.

To her unbounded credit, my sister, Audrey, has faithfully carried on this ministry for many years. It can be discouraging work because the average congregation is very small and the facilities meager, yet at eighty-five years of age (at this writing) she still faithfully preaches the Gospel. Faithfulness of this sort is in short supply these days. In our own ministry we have seen a decline in loyalty. Long-term service is less common than it used to be and people tend to do what pleases them rather than putting service for the Lord first and arranging their affairs around it.

Regardless of the limitations, I was delighted to be given an opportunity to preach. God's call was still clear in my mind and now a door had opened whereby I could begin to fulfill it. Our van being unreliable, a friend graciously lent me his motor bike and by this means I visited the various villages in the circuit. It was a dull time for Edna because she and the children could not all fit on the motor bike and had to remain at home.

Services were different in those tiny churches. There was usually a pedal (pump) organ and someone to play it. Talent varied considerably from church to church but we got by. There was sometimes no heating and in the winter the congregation sometimes sat in overcoats and gloves to keep warm. A smell of dampness pervaded most of the buildings and in some, stains on the walls bore silent testimony to the condition of the roof.

Excitement did sometimes liven up the scene however. On one occasion I was due to preach in the chapel just below our house. The people had congregated and we were about to begin the service when someone came in and said, "Mr. Day, your yearlings are all out in the road". With that, the entire congregation jumped to their feet and left the church to help me corral the yearlings. This was not easy because the hedges on either side of the road made it difficult to get ahead of them. If care was not taken they could run for miles. Someone had to jump over the hedge into the field, run ahead of the animals and then jump back into the road to head them off. The local children were expert at this and it was not long before the yearlings were safely back in captivity. We then went back into the chapel and conducted the service as if nothing had happened.

This lay ministry was wonderful training. I had been called to preach and at last I was filling my call. We had no idea what the future held but God did and He was in the process of preparing me for the ministry to come. We started a youth group in our tiny parlor. A surprisingly large number of kids from the surrounding farms turned up and we had some good times together, even putting on a play once, which was attended by local people from far and wide. The old chapel had not seen such excitement for decades!

As time passed, progress was made at Highertown. We were blessed with a good crop of lambs and good hay yields. We picked up an ancient tractor at a farm sale, which eased the work load greatly. We even added some fine North Devon steers. I was promoted again at the clay works and given charge of one of the pump houses. This eased our financial worries a little. It was pleasant to come in out of the weather and spend most of my time indoors where it was dry. The only times I needed to leave my shelter was when a stone became jammed in the feed pipe of the pump. Then I had to wade into the "pool" and pry it out.

Before leaving London I had read two books on organic farming by Newman Turner and had been impressed by his account of fertile fields, heavy hay crops and healthy livestock. On going to Highertown I decided to try his methods there. There was a big difference between the rich soil of Somerset, where he lived, and the shallow, peaty ground of the high moors, but I wrote to Mr. Turner for advice and he replied that he thought his method should still work there. I therefore sent away for seed containing a mixture of deep-rooted herbs, such as chicory. The local farmers rolled their eyes and considered such an experiment as being typical of what an ignorant "towny" might do. However, later they were obliged to admit it had paid off. When their fields went brown due to lack of rain, ours remained green. And when harvest time arrived our crop was abundant.

Nevertheless, there were strange phenomena connected to the soil up there on the moors. There was a cobalt deficiency that produced peculiar behavior in the sheep. Generally speaking, sheep and lambs born and raised in our area brought high prices at market because they were strong and used to inclement weather. However, the deficiency in the soil, though only a trace element, eventually caused the animals to behave unnaturally. We would find them chewing pieces of wood and their wool would begin to deteriorate. The problem was well-known in the area and every year the flocks had to be taken to the other side of the stream that marked our boundary for a just a week. If this were done, they would remain healthy for the remainder of the year. Upon crossing the stream, the sheep would begin to eat the grass ravenously, as if they knew it contained what they lacked. It was amazing to see how such a very small deficiency in the grass would make such a large difference in the sheep's welfare.

Despite the apparent improvement in our situation, the old green van eventually gave up the ghost and we were left without any transportation except for the borrowed motor bike. It was time to do something about it, so one day I rode into town and found a 1936 Austin seven. This was undoubtedly the smallest model car on the road but it was a car. At last we were able to squeeze the whole family into it and drive off together. Motors were simple in those days. Four cylinders, a battery, a coil, a carburetor and a distributor comprised the sum of gadgets under the hood, and although I had to start the car with a crank we found it a joy. The windshield wiper worked from the vacuum valve on the carburetor, so that it functioned very quickly going down hill and almost stopped going up. We always hoped the rain would ease by the time we reached an upward grade.

On June 24th, 1958 our third daughter, Nicola Jane, arrived. She came into the world upstairs in our bedroom, with a district health nurse in attendance. Earlier Edna had been taken by ambulance to the hospital in Plymouth because the nurse suspected she was carrying twins. However, tests showed this was not the case and she was brought home again. The district nurse was pleasant and efficient. When the time came for baby to arrive I called her very late in the day from the red phone box down the road and she willingly came to the house, complete with gas-and-air equipment and all other necessary tools. The only thing I had to supply was light (by means of a pumped-up pressure lamp) and hot water. I boiled a great deal of water during the next few hours, most of which proved to be unnecessary. During the event Jenny and Alyson slept peacefully in the next room. After what seemed to be an interminable time, Nicky made her appearance, weighing nine pounds (probably the result of the cream Fanny had been giving us) and looking rather like an Eskimo. Her mop of black hair gave her this appearance and we called her "Eskimo Nell". Next morning, the girls were intrigued to meet their new baby sister and were then taken to their grandma's house for a few days. Mrs. Turner, in the cottage across the road kindly took care of our washing and our other neighbor, Ioni (Ooni) Hicks, brought us meals. Both gestures were very much appreciated.

Neighbors

Our neighbors at the farm (the Hicks family) were particularly helpful during those years. Mr. Hicks Senior became an advisor to me. I remember sharing with him how I would like to get hold of more land so I could earn a full living from farming. He looked at me silently for a moment, leaning on the gate and chewing a piece of grass. Then he said, "Now look dear, you learn to farm the little one well first!" His advice remained with me and in later years I have used it in teaching others. I soon learned to respect him for his quiet grip of all things to do with the land and livestock.

Mr. Hicks had a brother, Stan, who farmed a small acreage across the valley. He was a strange old fellow with a brusque manner that could turn you away if you didn't know him. He had a bad leg and leaned heavily on a knobby stick. Nevertheless, he moved around in his fields, tending his livestock as if there were nothing wrong with him. I saw the softer side of him during lambing season one year. It was a cold, early spring night, quite dark, and one of our ewes was having a bad time. It was a breach birth. Sensing something was wrong, Stan came in quietly, holding up his lantern, and without saying anything he knelt down in the straw, washed his hands with some carbolic soap he had brought with him and set about delivering the lamb. When he had finished he got up, picked up his lantern, nodded a goodnight and quietly disappeared into the darkness.

After the senior Hicks retired and went to live down in Tresinney, their son, Lon and his wife Ione occupied the farm. We came to love the Hicks family and although the senior members of the family have long since left this earth, we have kept in touch with the younger ones to the present day. It was Lon who was responsible for getting me the job at the clay works. He worked the scrape there, scooping up the sand and rock from the pit bed. Sadly, he also has now gone and only his wife, Ione, survives.

CHAPTER 6

Immigration

In the Spring of 1959 we received a letter that would change the direction of our lives yet again. Looking back, we can see it was all in the Lord's plan but at the time we were not sure. The letter came from Olive, Edna's eldest sister, who lived in Milwaukee, Wisconsin. Olive had married a GI after the war and had immigrated to the United States. In her letter, Olive suggested that we join them there in Milwaukee. She said they would be willing to sponsor us and we should be able to find work when we arrived. With her letter she sent along some magazines illustrating life in the US.

At first we were shaken by the idea. It was such a big step to take and immigration had never entered our minds. For my part, I had no desire to leave the land and go to America. I loved the sweet air and freedom of our fields, even though we were decidedly short on luxuries. My imaginary view of America (born out of the movies) with its huge cars, gangsters and chromium-plated soda fountains, did not appeal to me at all. However, we wanted to be obedient to the Lord so we made a covenant. We would apply for a visa (which in those days was difficult to secure) and if we were successful we would go to America in faith. We prayed earnestly that the Lord's will would be done. We asked Him to not allow the visa to be granted unless He had a specific plan for us. I believe this incident brought us one step closer in our relationship with the Lord. It was with trepidation that we completed the forms and mailed them to the United States embassy in London.

Our prayer was answered more promptly than we expected. A letter from the embassy arrived shortly setting a date for us to attend for an interview. This meant a drive to London in our tiny car, which presented quite a challenge. We hastily arranged to stay with my grandmother overnight and when the day arrived we bundled the kids into the back seat of our Austin Seven and set out for the capital. The weather was good and although the journey was much longer than anything we had attempted in this vehicle before, we arrived in London without incident.

The embassy, in Grosvenor Square, was bustling with other applicants, slowly moving through the same process as ourselves. When our turn came, we answered questions, signed forms and were sent to another address, not far from the embassy, where we waited our turn to have chest x-rays. Each wait was quite long and the problem of keeping a six year-old, a three-year old and a one-year old occupied during that time was quite an assignment. Our turn eventually came but Edna's x-ray showed old scar tissue on her lung (probably dating back to the pneumonia she had suffered as a small child) and we had to wait a second time until her x-ray could be reevaluated. To our relief, the doctors finally decided that the scar tissue indicated no current problem and we were cleared. We then had to return to the embassy and wait our turn again. Having presented our clearance from the doctor we were told to take a seat and wait again for our name to be called. Most of the day had passed by this time but finally we were called and rewarded with our visas. The decision was now made. God had answered our prayer and visas had been issued. We were committed to immigrate! We piled back into the car and drove to my grandmother's house in Blackheath, where we were able to recover from the day's ordeal.

It was strange to return to work and tell my co-workers that we were going to America. America seemed so unfamiliar, so far away. Just hearing ourselves say it sounded unreal. Worse still, we had to break the news to our parents. Mine did not react kindly. They (especially my mother) felt we were deserting them. In reality I suppose we were, but we didn't want them to feel rejected. Edna's parents looked upon the news differently. They had visited Milwaukee during an official visit to America while Dad was mayor of Reading and they already had a daughter living there. The idea was therefore not as radical to them as it was to my parents, who had never crossed the Atlantic.

Preparing to leave

The next step was to sell up everything. The livestock, furniture, household items, all had to go because we could only take what we could carry (five suitcases – one per person). There was an emotional aspect to this because we could not expect to receive much from the sale of used items, yet they had a sentimental value to us. Many of them had been with us since we were married and seeing them carried away by strangers felt rather like a violation of our privacy. Ray, our brother-in-law in Milwaukee, came through for us, submitting the sponsorship papers and guaranteeing us a place to stay. The US authorities wanted to make sure we would not end up on the street and insisted on a guarantee of support. He also lent us the money to buy our tickets and after a comparatively short but traumatic time we were ready to leave for the unknown.

My father took over our little car and the day came when we locked the door of the cottage and went to my parents' house in preparation for our train journey to London. Farewells are never pleasant but they had to be said and on about the 14th October, 1959, we found ourselves on the train, surrounded by suitcases, on the first leg of our journey. Edna's Mum and Dad, in Reading, received us and there we awaited the time of our departure from Heathrow airport. Due to bad weather, the flight was delayed several times. In those days, airlines were more attentive to their passengers' needs than they are today and we received several telephone calls telling us of the delays. Eventually we were notified that the flight was cleared and we all piled into Edna's parents' van and drove to Heathrow. We still had to wait there for a considerable time but the gate was finally opened and we were allowed through.

In those days boarding always took place out on the tarmac. After bidding farewell to Edna's family we walked out into the drizzly night and climbed the steps into our plane. It was a four-engined, propeller driven, Lockheed "Constellation" which looked enormous to us. The seats inside were arranged in two rows of twos, one row on either side of a center aisle. Edna sat beside Alyson with Nicky on her lap and I sat with Jenny. Alyson fought against having her seat belt fastened, which began the journey rather badly for Edna, but once everyone was seated, the door was closed and we took off into the night on our big adventure. Leaving the dull drizzle on the ground, we climbed up through the clouds blanketing London and suddenly burst out into an enchanted world. A full moon, shining in a clear sky, painted the clouds below in silver. This beautiful scene stretched into the distance as far as we could see. People on the ground looked up at the same clouds and grumbled about the miserable weather, while we looked down on them and marveled at their serenity and beauty. Life itself is often like that. When days are dark and the light is shut out, there is always beauty on the other side.

The night drew on and the passengers fell asleep. I had difficulty sleeping for two reasons. The first was that my seat was situated behind the wing of the aircraft and the engines sent out flames into the darkness. This was an uncomfortable sight for someone unused to flying. However, after a while, when we failed to crash, I came to the realization that this was a normal phenomenon. The second reason for my sleeplessness was that terrible doubts assailed me. I looked at Edna and the children sleeping and I thought: "You fool! What have you done? You have given up your job in England and you have none to go to in America. You have no idea what awaits you there. Talk about irresponsibility! Edna and the children trust you and rely upon you and you are taking them six thousand miles from their homeland with no guarantee for the future!" For the time being I had forgotten that we had prayed about our decision and that God had answered our prayer by opening the way. I spent an uncomfortable night, feeling alone and miserable above the Atlantic Ocean.

Introduction to the New World

It was light again when we approached New York. Out of our window we caught our first glimpse of America and began to ready ourselves to leave the aircraft. When we stepped off the plane the awaiting scene was far from romantic. The usual worn and dirty airport buildings confronted us and we were herded into the lobby to collect our bags. Having retrieved these, we then had to go through Immigration and Customs. Our plane was many hours late in arriving and our connection to Milwaukee had long since departed. I left Edna with the bags and went to enquire about another flight. When I returned she and the children seemed to be under arrest. They were cornered in a little glass booth, while men with guns (something we had never seen in England) were examining our cases. This was a bad omen because we already had a guilty conscience.

We knew we were not supposed to bring antiques into the country but we had included an ancient pewter tankard in our luggage because it was special to us. We had purchased it on one of our early trips together. As soon as I saw the police around our luggage I "knew" that they were after the tankard. They passed some kind of detector (which I assumed to be an antique detector) over the suitcase and, sure enough, they pulled out our contraband item. However, they seemed uninterested in the tankard itself but instead pulled out some socks stuffed inside, and wrapped in the socks they found a boy scout's compass that I was bringing for one of the kids. The magnetic needle had evidently set off a warning. The policeman held up the tankard in his hand and said to Edna, "What are you going to do with this? Make tea in it?" and with a good natured grin popped the tankard back into the suitcase. That was our introduction to New York and we breathed a sigh of relief when we found ourselves on the far side of the barrier with all our documents approved.

A bus took us from Idlewild to LaGuardia airfield to catch our connection. Things went smoothly there and within an hour or two we were landing in Milwaukee. Due to our flight's long delay, Olive and her husband had gone home, thinking we were not coming. We telephoned them and waited in the airfield lobby until they returned for us. Olive and Edna were delighted to see one another again. Ray shook my hand and solemnly said, "Welcome to America". We then loaded our luggage into his station wagon and started on our journey to their house. What seemed strange to me was that throughout the journey he did not once change gears. It was almost as if he remained in first gear all the way, and yet the engine did not race. It was my first introduction to an automatic transmission. I had never seen, or heard of such a thing before. This, of course, was to be the first in a long list of new things we would encounter in the weeks ahead.

Shorewood, Wisconsin

Ray and Olive lived in Shorewood, a community on the shore of Lake Michigan to the north of Milwaukee. Beautiful old houses and mature trees lined the streets. Coming as we had directly from Highertown, the opulence of the area impressed us. We would go out for walks in the evenings and catch glimpses of the brightly lit interiors of some of the big houses. The house in which we had come to live was not a mansion but it was a fine old home with spacious rooms and accommodation sufficient to house the five of us in addition to Olive's seven. The evening we arrived I accompanied Ray on a visit to the local supermarket. This was entrance into a different world. I had seen nothing approaching the size of the store or abundance of items for sale. In England we had shopped in small local stores, where we asked at the counter for the items we needed and carried them away in a basket. The idea of pushing a cart around this enormous, brightly lit space, helping one's self to whatever was needed and then having an employee load it into multiple brown paper bags, was a new and somewhat overwhelming experience.

Edna writes: "I was delighted to be reunited with my sister, Olive, and her family but I was overwhelmed by the luxury of her home, in particular the kitchen and bathroom. Ray (an interior decorator by trade) had recently remodeled the kitchen. The walls were lined with the latest cream colored metal cabinets and there were actually *two* ovens, an upper and a lower one! The strange noise I heard from time to time came from the garbage disposal. It seemed (and was) thousands of miles from our humble home on the Cornish moors. It truly was a new beginning -- so many things to get used to, new sights, sounds, smells, food, words, customs. Our children were also delighted to be with their cousins but like us, felt overwhelmed by their new surroundings. At times we felt like refugees. Ashley, bless his heart, didn't even wait for the jet lag to be over. The very next day he was out checking out job situations."

Everything was new to us. Food, bathroom fittings, window and door catches, light switches and customs in general all seemed strange. Each day was an adventure. The day after our arrival I searched the newspaper for jobs. I was attracted by an advertisement placed by the Washington National Insurance Company for someone to train as an agent. No experience was required. I telephoned the office and was granted an interview. After waiting for the city bus, I climbed aboard and sat down on a side seat near the driver. After a moment he said in a loud voice, "What about your fare, bud?" I was used to a conductor coming round for the fares but I assumed I had to pay him, so I got up and offered him some money. He pointed to a box beside him so I threw in the money and some coins came out. I picked these up, thinking they were my change. A moment or two later, the driver said again, "What about your fare, bud?" Now I was really confused. I had given him my money, received my change and he still wanted more! A kindly lady next to me explained that the machine had simply changed my large coin into smaller ones. Now I had to place my fare into the box. I thanked her profusely and did as she said. This time the driver seemed satisfied and I explained to my benefactor that this was my first day in America. She seemed quite excited by my revelation and instructed me more fully on the mysteries of riding American public transportation.

The interview at the Washington National went very well. I was told I had to undergo some psychological testing but if that proved acceptable I had the job. Next day I was tested and was evidently pronounced sane because I started work the following day. My work mates were very friendly but unusual. Both were Jewish and both had stories to tell. One had been in Auschwitz during the war and had escaped death only because he could play the piano and was used by the guards to entertain them. The other came from Holland and had spent the war years hiding in an attic high above the street. Having immigrated himself, Rudi (the Dutchman) saw my need and immediately took me to a men's outfitters, where he purchased for me a suit and a hat because the clothes I had were of a different style and rather conspicuous in American society. He understood, and I was always grateful for Rudi's kindness.

Village Missions

There followed a week or two of training, at the end of which I was ready to sit for the insurance agent's examination. Having passed this I was sent out on my own to sell insurance. The company serviced the insurance program for public health nurses and I was given a handful of cards to follow up. One bitterly cold evening I called at the home of a nurse named Helen Sellner, who had requested information. We talked about insurance but she had another topic in mind. She asked me about my background and when I told her of my call to preach and my experience in rural Cornwall she announced that I was definitely in the wrong business. She said I should be preaching the Gospel in rural America instead of selling insurance in Milwaukee. She explained she had been involved in a mission called "Village Missions" which supplied pastors to small rural churches. She said the need was great, that many congregations were seeking help and that I would fit perfectly into the role. I sold her an insurance policy that evening but she "sold" me something far more important. She sent me home with literature about Village Missions and my interest was stimulated. Edna and I read the material she had given me and talked for a long time about the possibilities. We both felt drawn to the work but God's time had not yet arrived.

Edna adds: "Shortly after reading the literature regarding Village Missions, I had a vivid dream. In my dream I was standing before the Lord and He held in His hand the book of my life. As He flipped over the pages, I realized they were mostly blank. Just here and there was an entry. I understood that the entries marked times when I had been a witness for Him. As I looked up into His eyes, filled with such love and compassion, I was overcome with regret and shame. I knew that because of fear and nervousness I had kept my faith a secret. How relieved and thankful I was, when I awoke next morning, to find that I had not died but was still alive and had more time to serve my Lord. I fell on my knees by the bed and asked God's forgiveness. Then I claimed the verse in Philippians 4:13, "I can do all things through Christ who strengthens me". I believe with all my heart that this was God's way of assuring me of His call for me to become a pastor's wife."

It is strange, but I can still see the picture that came into my mind when Edna and I read about Village Missions. In my imagination I was walking down an old sidewalk with uneven paving stones and big maple trees overshadowing it. Beside the sidewalk a tall iron fence marked the boundary to a private yard and brightly colored Autumn leaves covered the ground. The field to which we were eventually sent was nothing like this picture. It had no sidewalks at all, the trees were all pines and there was not an iron fence within a twenty mile radius! Nevertheless, the mental picture was clear and to this day I can still see it in my mind.

At the end of my visit with Mrs. Sellner I asked her to suggest names of others who might be interested in insurance. This was standard procedure. She was quite willing and provided several, all of whom where active Christians. When I called one of them to ask for an interview, she told me she would be pleased to meet with me but it would have to be after the Wednesday Bible study at the Church of the Open Door. This, of course, was part of her plan to bring me under the sound of the Gospel. She had no idea I was already a Christian. I was happy to comply and found the study was in Hebrews 7, which describes the nature of the mysterious Melchisedek. The depth of the study intrigued me and I wanted to know more about the church. This was Helen Sellner's purpose in choosing the names she gave me. Thus we were introduced to the Body which would later support us throughout our service with Village Missions.

In retrospect, the hand of the Lord is unmistakable. It was not coincidence that led me to apply to the Washington National Insurance Company for employment. It was not coincidence that this particular company happened to service the Public Health Nurses' insurance plan. It was not coincidence that had me knocking on Helen Sellner's door during my first few days of selling, nor that she was a strong advocate of Village Missions and was interested enough to probe into my background.

Nor was it coincidence that, through contact with Helen, Edna and I were introduced to the church that was to support us throughout our later service with the mission. God had it all under control and began implementing His plan the day after we landed in the United States!

First Months in America

A month after our arrival in America the presidency of Dwight Eisenhower, who had served as supreme allied commander during the European war, came to an end and our first American presidential Election took place. The process was quite different from those we had witnessed in England. There, the leader of the victorious party (the party with the most seats in Parliament) automatically becomes prime minister. In the States, of course, the people vote for the president (in this case John F. Kennedy) directly. Thus, we began our lives in the USA under the leadership of a new president.

By this time we had taken possession of an apartment near Olive and had settled in comfortably. Edna said she could not stand the taste (or even the smell) of American (Franz) bread, that it made her feel sick. Other things seemed to make her sick as well and we soon realized that baby number four was on the way. It was not easy for Edna to be pregnant so soon after our arrival in a new country but she coped very well.

Having settled into the apartment, we also became the proud owners of a beautiful Plymouth car. It was powder blue with gold trim and had an electronic transmission. It was difficult at first to push buttons instead of manipulating a gear lever, but we soon became used to it. We really enjoyed this car, driving out along the beach front on Sunday afternoons and buying ice cream at one of the stalls along the way.

As time passed, the Washington National decided that my period of training was complete. The supply of request cards dried up and I was supposed to find my own prospects. This was difficult for me. I had made a record number of sales while the contact cards had been supplied but I found it extremely difficult to pry the names and addresses of friends from people and then try to sell them insurance. I would not like this to happen to me and I found it difficult to inflict it on others. The result was that sales rapidly dwindled. As I look back, I can see that God was controlling the circumstances. He had used the company as part of His plan and did not wish me to succeed in the insurance business (or at anything else for that matter) because He had a different purpose planned for Edna and me.

Because God is sovereign He is obviously never frustrated but if I had been in His place, I think I would have been frustrated by our tardiness in recognizing His plan. I cannot explain why we took so long before applying to Village Missions. We recognized its value and I think we saw ourselves as part of it eventually, but for some reason we delayed taking the plunge. In our defense, we were still new to the country and our fourth child was due quite soon. We knew nothing outside the immediate confines of Milwaukee and were still a little bewildered by the newness of everything. Perhaps this was what delayed our decision.

I finally gave notice at the Washington National and became a representative for the Dale Carnegie Sales Course. This amounted to a bunch of psychological hoo-hah, designed to get people excited about selling. I attained super-high grades when taking the course myself but when it came to selling it to others I failed dismally. I was supposed to go round the city, visiting businesses and persuading management that their representatives needed this course to increase sales. Most of them disagreed with me and my success was minimal. The truth was that I didn't believe in the product myself and my lack of conviction must have come through.

While I was taking the Dale Carnegie course, I met a real estate man named Robert Johnson. He convinced me that it was better business to buy a house than to rent one. The result was that we purchased a house on Milwaukee's south side (3584 S. Quincey Avenue) for $14,500. It was a row house but very comfortable and well appointed. Heat was piped into the floor and there was adequate room for our growing family. In addition, it fronted on to a large public playing field, which offered plenty of playing room for the children. In the winter an area was flooded and turned into a skating rink. Jenny and Alyson were duly fitted with ice skates and made their debut on the ice. Jenny ventured out carefully, making sure she didn't over reach herself but Alyson plunged into the project with careless abandon, arms and legs flying, determined to be an expert skater by the end of the first session! It was interesting to see the different personalities demonstrated so clearly, even at that young age.

Milwaukee Rescue Mission

Inevitably, the time came when I left Dale Carnegie. Once again I was out of work, which was not a good feeling. Everyone around me seemed to be happily employed but if one is without visible means of support a cold ache settles in the stomach and a sense of fear lurks in the shadows. I went to the pastor to tell him my woes. Sensing that I really needed Christian involvement he mentioned that one of the church members was the director of the Milwaukee Rescue Mission. Perhaps he could help. Thanking him, I went along to the mission and discovered they were looking for a book-keeper. I had never done book-keeping but I had once read a book entitled "Anybody Can Do Anything" and so I offered my services. Miraculously I was given the job. I rushed over to a nearby book store, bought a book on book-keeping and filled the time before my starting date swatting the subject!

Life at the Rescue Mission was interesting. I successfully kept the books, preached sometimes and received groups from the churches round about who came to conduct services. It was fulfilling work. Very occasionally we encountered a difficult individual but for the most part everything ran smoothly. I was amazed to see the havoc that alcohol can play in a person's life. We had doctors, lawyers, teachers and all kinds of professional men who had lost everything and were now on the street due to alcoholism. It was difficult to imagine how far a person can fall once he is taken over by addiction. Another pathetic experience was seeing men who had been delivered from drinking and who had remained sober for a long time, suddenly fall back and be overcome. Some of the staff members were recovering alcoholics.

They were employed on the condition that they remained sober. If they relapsed they forfeited their position. We saw several who had worked at the mission for a long time lose their privileges in this way. Employment at the mission meant parting with our beautiful blue Plymouth because the small salary put the running of any kind of car out of reach. Nevertheless, we were content. It was good to be serving the Lord instead of struggling in the secular arena.

On August 2nd, 1960, Edna was admitted to Mount Sinai Hospital for the delivery of our fourth daughter, Jillian Mary. It was a hot day and a thunder storm threatened. Dr. Schwartz, the attending physician had gone to some kind of banquet and arrived at the hospital in evening dress. He was not cross, however, and treated Edna with great kindness. This time I was able to stay with her until the showdown actually came. Then I was expelled and waited for what seemed an eternity in the waiting room. Eventually the doctor emerged and announced that a beautiful baby girl had been born and I could go in and see them. I was surprised to find that, unlike the others, our new daughter had a mop of auburn hair. To the casual observer this was strange, considering both Edna and I were dark. However, closer examination revealed that all of the children had red lights in their hair, as also did Edna. And when I grew my first beard at Highertown it had come out red! Jillian obviously carried the auburn genes but exhibited them a little more obviously than the rest of us.

As I left the hospital that night an almighty thunder storm erupted. Thunder storms in the mid-west are quite unlike those experienced on the west coast. Flashes of lightening and peals of thunder continue incessantly, like a military bombardment, and rain falls in sheets. Thus Jillian was heralded in a very dramatic way but by the time Edna and Jillian came home all was peace and sunshine once again.

CHAPTER 7

Redland, Oregon

Village Missions Becomes a Reality

Life at the rescue mission became routine. I was happy enough there but always felt that God had something more for me. Then one day in the Fall of 1961 Helen Sellner told us that a Christian Women's Club conference was to take place in Chicago a month or so later and that the director of Village Missions, Walter Duff, would be present. She pointed out that if I had any desire to serve with Village Missions this would be an excellent opportunity to meet the director. Having prayed about it, Edna and I felt drawn to take the step. I therefore sent for application documents and duly submitted them to the home office. A short time later, a letter of confirmation came from the mission, agreeing to set up an appointment with Mr. Duff at the Chicago conference. Mrs. Sellner arranged the appointment and accompanied me to Chicago to make the introduction.

When we arrived at the site of the conference, a village missionary was speaking to a packed house. I listened to him while Mrs. Sellner went to find Mr. Duff. What he said excited me. He was telling the group about his work and the people whose lives had been transformed when they received Christ as their Savior. I was strangely moved and suddenly wanted above all else to become part of the work.

Soon Mrs. Sellner returned with Mr. Duff and an introduction was made. She then retired, leaving me to speak to the director alone. In his boyhood he had come to the States from Ireland. As a matter of interest, he and his family were actually booked on the Titanic but for some reason their mother changed ships at the last moment. The Lord had work for them to do. Due to his own upbringing in Ireland he was able to appreciate my education and preaching experience. He knew from my application where we had been and what we had done. He asked many questions and seemed satisfied with my answers. Finally, he said he would take me on, even though I had never attended Bible school. He considered the training and experience I had received in England adequately equipped me to become a village missionary. I could not wait to tell Edna the good news.

Edna adds: "Soon after our acceptance into the mission we were invited to speak at the Milwaukee Christians Women's Club as new representatives of Village Missions. Both Ashley and I were asked to speak!! It was a very large club and I can still remember the huge room filled with beautifully dressed women. There were at least four hundred present. I wore a borrowed dress from my sister, Olive, not owning a suitable one of my own."

"As we were escorted to the "top table" to be seated, my old fears of public speaking began to overwhelm me. The meal was served but my appetite had disappeared. The meeting moved along and the president of the club began to explain to the audience the work of Village Missions. I heard her say my name as being next on the program. Offering up a silent prayer I took my notes in my hand and stood to my feet. As if in a dream, I remembered the verse which I had claimed when Jesus had appeared to me: "I can do all things through Christ who strengthens me" (Philippians 4:13). As I opened my mouth to speak it was as though God's peace washed over me, from the top of my head throughout my whole being. I stopped shaking and my words were clear. God seemed to give me each one. What a lesson to me of God's amazing faithfulness! I knew then that I could go in confidence, not in myself but in Him."

There were now preparations to be made. First, we purchased a big Buick car from a man in the Rescue mission who had lost his license to drive. It was old but in great condition. Then we placed the house on the market. It sold for $1,000 less than we had paid for it. Finally we arranged to sell everything we could not carry. Since coming to America we had accumulated some nice items of furniture but for the second time, Edna saw her home piled unceremoniously onto a second-hand dealer's truck and carted away. Village Missions told us we had to be ready to go to either coast. We were not to take any furniture because the people on the field would furnish a house for us. The Church of the Open Door was wonderful. They rallied round us, prayed for us and pledged to cover our entire support requirements. Then one evening a group visited our house and left behind a sizeable money gift when they departed. A man in the church helped me to construct a wooden luggage rack that fitted on top of the car and eventually we were ready to leave. Fairly deep snow covered the ground but we bundled the kids into warm clothes and packed them in the back seat of the car.

The first leg of our journey took us to Kansas City, Missouri, where the headquarters of Village Missions, a campus known as Stonecroft, is located. Stonecroft consisted of an old mansion, surrounded by newer, buildings, in which the staff lived and worked. The grounds were beautiful. An avenue of mature trees led to the big house and gardens surrounded many of the buildings. Orchards supplied fruit in their season. Since we were coming to Stonecroft "on approval" we wanted to make the best possible impression. However, just as we drew up outside the big house Nicky threw up over the back of Edna's seat. Later she managed to lock herself in the bathroom, which created another disturbance. However, management and staff were most gracious and our dramatic introduction seemed not to downgrade us very much in their eyes.

Stonecroft is actually the headquarters of Christian Women's Clubs of America and Christian Business and Professional Women's Clubs. These clubs meet monthly in towns and cities all over America and in many other countries of the world. Their founder was a woman named Helen Baugh. Along the way she joined forces with a partner, named Mary Clark and these two directed the work from just a few small meetings to the world organization it now is. Each club meets for lunch in an hotel. After lunch there is a special feature, where someone demonstrates a craft or skill and then a speaker gives a message or testimony in which the way of salvation is clearly presented. Many women have come to know the Lord through these meetings.

Throughout the years of their existence, the two women's clubs have supported Village Missions. Many communities in which either the church has closed or where there are insufficient funds to support a pastor have received help from the organization. Vision for the ministries began at the beginning of the 20th century, when the founding family immigrated to the United States from Ireland. The children were all leaders in their own right and over a period of time they each founded and directed their own ministry. Helen Baugh founded the women's clubs, Walter Duff (her brother) directed Village Missions and Evangeline McNeill (their sister) directed the Canon Beach Conference Center. The family was thus responsible for a very large, divergent and effective ministry. All have now gone to be with the Lord and their work is being carried on by others.

Although Mr. Duff operated out of his home in Dallas, Oregon, the headquarters of Village Missions was actually Stonecroft. From there administration for all the ministries was coordinated. It was to this complex that we had now been summoned in order to await our assignment to a field.

For several days we were put to work around the campus. Among other things, I tiled a bathroom and swept out the conservatory. We learned later that this was policy. They wanted to see if we were willing to do menial tasks without complaining. All the time we wondered where they would send us, since no destination had yet been mentioned or even hinted at. I remember walking in the grove of big trees along the driveway and praying. I said, "Lord, it doesn't matter where you send us. We are ready to go wherever you will. But if it please you, could you send us to a place where there is something beautiful?" It was probably a selfish prayer but I think the Lord understood.

Redland, Oregon

A day or so later we were summoned to the office. They told us that Mr. Duff had called and had assigned us to a place called Redland, in Oregon. He said the people there would be expecting us and we should set out as soon as possible. With great excitement we studied the map, to see where Redland was, and then gathered our things together and packed up the car. We filled the well in front of the back seat with suitcases and then piled bedding on top to make a platform level with the seat. This provided Alyson and Jennie and Nicky with a large, soft area on which to sit or lie at will. Seat belts had not yet made their debut and Jillian sat on Edna's lap in the front seat. This was not ideal because Edna suffered from car sickness in those days and Jillian's wriggling presence did nothing to improve the problem. After prayer next morning, February 16th, 1962, the Stonecroft staff sent us off on our big adventure. Eighteen hundred and fifty miles of unexplored country now lay ahead of us. We had never been west of Kansas City and coming from a small country like England the distance between us and Oregon seemed vast and mysterious.

The first part of our journey was not easy due to the heavy snow that had fallen in Missouri. At one point we hit a snowdrift that had formed across the road. Snow flew in all directions but we were heavy enough to break through and continue on our way. After a while we drove out of the snow and were relieved to find ourselves on dry pavement. Soon we crossed the Missouri border into Kansas and then into Wyoming. The vast stretches of empty prairie amazed us. We seemed to drive for hours and hours without getting anywhere. We wondered if Oregon would be like this and hoped it would not be. The modern motels we know today had not yet made their appearance. We stayed in little cabins clustered round a center court. They were primitive but warm and provided safe lodging for the night.

As we neared the western side of Wyoming we saw the Rocky Mountains rising in the distance and soon we were negotiating the snowy mountain passes. All this was new to us and although we admired the scenery we felt over-awed by the size of the peaks that now surrounded us. They made us feel insignificant and lonely as we made our way among them.

Crossing into southern Idaho we followed the Snake river canyon with the river rushing along its base. This eventually brought us out into dry grassy hills near Boise that looked as if they were covered with velvet. Once across Idaho we finally reached Oregon and driving north into the Blue Mountains we stopped for the night in La Grande. Next morning, dropping down from the high country through the pine forest, we caught our first glimpse of the Columbia River. In 1962 the present freeway had not yet been built and so we followed the twisty road beside the water for miles. Sometimes it would wind through beautiful mossy wooded areas, where water falls cascaded down from above. At others it would pass beneath gigantic cliffs that rose straight up from the road. Tunnels cut through some of these cliffs enabled trains to make their way. The kids liked to wave to the man in the caboose, who would wave back to them. We have driven along the Columbia River Gorge many times since that day but have never lost our appreciation of its majestic beauty.

After an ice cream stop at Multnomah Falls, we were soon in Portland and finding our way along the Willamette to Oregon City. From there a narrow road twisted toward Redland and we knew we were within shouting distance of our destination. We pulled in by the roadside, combed our hair, washed the kids faces with spit and attempted to look as ministerial as possible. A mile or two more, a sharp left by the local store and we had arrived. A little white church stood on the top of a grassy bank with a steeple pointing skywards. A lady emerged and introduced herself as the mission representative. She then waved us on up the road to the parsonage. Only the village school and the parsonage shared this road, which ended in the school gates. When school was out it was therefore very quiet and secluded. Everything was compact. School, church, house and store were all within a few hundred yards of one another.

Edna writes: "How good the Lord is in His provision. The thing that amazes me is His total knowledge of us and of our individual needs. He knew that at that time I had never learned to drive a car and He lovingly placed us where I had no need to do so."

The parsonage was a shingle-clad ranch house, standing foursquare beside the road. Inside there were three bedrooms, a small living room, a kitchen, bathroom and basement -- but no furniture! We looked around us and wondered what we were going to sleep on, sit on or eat on. Mr. Duff had assured us the field would supply furnished accommodation and we had disposed of our own belongings with that understanding. We had been prepared for an old, even primitive house but not for an empty one! However, we knew the Lord had brought us this far and we believed He would take us the rest of the way. All we had to do was wait. Sure enough, within a short time people began to arrive bearing items of furniture. First, four people arrived, each bringing a rocking chair. This provided four rockers in the empty living room. The children were soon rocking energetically. Then a table and some folding chairs were brought in from the church to provide facilities for eating. Finally, some old iron bedsteads arrived with badly stained mattresses. Edna had misgivings about the children using these but for the time being, at least, we had no other choice.

Edna adds: "Fortunately we had packed our bed linens and blankets into the roomy well of our old Buick. The children had used the whole area on which to play and sleep on the journey over. The remainder of our essentials arrived a week or so later, packed in a wooden container made by the men at the rescue mission."

Eventually, the helpful and the curious went home, the children were put to bed and we were left alone to take stock of our situation. There was much to be grateful for. We had survived a long and eventful journey, there was a roof over our heads, a fire was burning in the furnace downstairs and although the house was very bare and very "un-cozy", at least it was a private place which we could improve as funds became available. Best of all, the desire God had put into our hearts back at Harringay Arena had finally been fulfilled. We were on our own mission field, with our little church just down the road! It was not quite as we had imagined but then reality never is. We soon made up a bed for ourselves and, tired from our trip, we slept like lambs.

Redland itself was very small. A filling station and local store comprised the "downtown" area. Private dwellings scattered among the fields and Filbert orchards made up the remainder of the community, which covered a wide area. It was a peaceful place with very little traffic and the local people seemed friendly. It was a niche where we could settle down, feel at home and begin our ministry.

Evergreen Community Church

A day or so later, on our first Sunday in Redland, a record group turned out to meet their new pastor and his family. The congregation was comprised mainly of older folk, though there were a few teenagers and children present. The church itself was a typical country building, rising to a high vaulted ceiling and smelling faintly of old wood and dry rot. The pews were not built for comfort and there was little danger of anyone dozing off during the service. Music was - well, loud! Everyone sang with gusto but the effect was not particularly melodious. Toilet facilities consisted of two outhouses in the gravel parking lot, one for the ladies and the other for the gentlemen. The piano was slightly out of tune but none of these things did anything to dampen our spirits. It was a strange but exhilarating experience to be preaching from a pulpit that was now officially "mine". Not that I owned it, or had any authority over it, but I had been given the privilege of being this body's spiritual leader, and I would be expected to preach from this pulpit every Sunday. My previous preaching experience had always been as a guest, arriving just before the service began and leaving immediately afterwards. By contrast, this was permanent. As I looked out across the congregation, I saw faces that would become very familiar to Edna and me over the next few years.

Early in the following week, the mist that had persisted since we arrived in Redland lifted. The sky became blue and the sun shone. Leaving our front door we looked across the wide valley and to our pleasure and surprise there, dominating the scene, was Mount Hood, gleaming white in the sunshine and rising majestically above the surrounding hills. It had been obscured by the mist until this point but now it was revealed in all its glory. I remembered my prayer in the driveway at Stonecroft, when I had asked the Lord for something beautiful to look at. Once again, He had done the "exceeding abundant" thing. In later years we conducted sunrise services on a church member's property overlooking

114

this valley. The sun came up right behind the mountain and provided a spectacular setting for our service.

As the weeks passed and we became accustomed to our new surroundings, life settled to a regular routine. Jennie and Alyson were enrolled at the school opposite and soon played happily with new friends. Nicky and Jill were still too young for school and remained at home with Edna. We began a youth ministry that met in our living room each week and before long this had grown to a sizeable group. In addition, once each week we held "Release Time" when the children at the school were all allowed to leave classes and come down to our church for one hour. There would be a time of singing followed by Bible stories illustrated by flannel graphs. This was a wonderful way to reach the local boys and girls with the Gospel. Though many of the children and their families did not attend church, nobody ever complained about the children being taught Scripture. Some parents began attending church as the result of their children enjoying Release Time.

Emergencies did arise from time to time. On one occasion, one of the boys failed to get up from the bench when it was time to go back to school. We soon discovered the reason. He had pushed his thumb through a knot hole in the bench on which he was sitting and was unable to pull it out. Several of us worked for some time on the problem, unsuccessfully, and eventually we had to carry the bench (with the boy attached) up to the school, where the woodwork teacher sawed him free.

The pillars of our congregation were nearly all farmers and each had a unique character. Before we left Stonecroft we were warned about one man who had a name for demanding his own way. He was reported as once saying (regarding the church): "If I can't run it I'll wreck it!" Thankfully, we never had any trouble with him. He was forceful and outspoken but he never caused us any problems. His farm was meticulously clean. There was never anything lying around or out of place. His yard was swept and immaculate and he expected the church to be run the same way. This was not always possible but he never disrupted the peace. After a while he became a strong supporter and even visited us after we moved away.

The secretary of the church (Mr. Lutz) was a rugged old German. His wife was the treasurer. They had lived in the Redland area and been members of the church for many years. Each New Year's Eve Mr. Lutz would show old home movies in the church basement. They were all about the people who were members of the congregation in days long gone by. It was fascinating to watch them arrive at the church in ancient cars and walk about with quick jerky steps due to the speed of the movie. Mr. Lutz's movies were always popular with the people.

Other members of that first church are indelibly recorded in our memories. There were Mr. and Mrs. Oppy, for instance, who drove a car almost as old as they were. The Oppy's had come from the Pentecostal persuasion and viewed our body as being somewhat reserved. They were a little more boisterous in their faith than we were but always supported the clear teaching of God's Word. They were both remarkable for their age and were prominent members.

Though the church gradually developed over time, it was very basic when we first arrived and still displayed the quaint characteristics of yesteryear. Two events impressed this upon us very forcefully. The first was the annual members' meeting that took place not many months after we arrived. Deacons were elected by the public vote of the congregation and the names of those nominated were written on a chalk board at the front of the church. As the votes were read out, a mark was placed beside the name chosen. This became embarrassing for those who received few votes. Mr. Oppy was regularly in charge of counting the votes and they were always collected in a special hat. On this occasion he had left the hat in his car and there was a delay in the proceedings while someone went to fetch it. The votes were duly collected in the hat but when Mr. Oppy came to read them he discovered he had forgotten to bring his glasses. Various members of the congregation offered him theirs and in a process of elimination he tried on each pair until he found one through which he could read the ballots. All this took place in solemn gravity but Edna and I had great difficulty in keeping our faces composed.

The other event that impressed upon us the quaintness of our little church was the talent show, which took place periodically. There was one lady who insisted on singing solos. She was tone deaf and the resultant performance was excruciating. Another old lady knew one poem about a little girl on a train. She recited it at every show and the congregation enthusiastically expressed their appreciation every time. It was as if we had dropped back in time to frontier days, yet we grew to love these folks, with their rough and ready ways and innocent lack of sophistication.

Slowly, people with more experience began to join us. The congregation grew in size and maturity and we were able to plan more adventurous things. A number trusted Christ as their Savior and others grew in their faith. In this little church I conducted my first communion service, my first funeral, my first wedding and my first baby dedication. Each of these was a traumatic experience because I had nothing to go on but my memory of how our old pastor in Wokingham had done it. However, the Lord was sufficient for my need and saw me through. Baptismal services were conducted in a beautiful private lake surrounded by trees. On one occasion we had a very large number of candidates.

I think one of the benefits of not having attended a theological establishment is that I am not stereotyped. I do things differently simply because nobody ever told me how they "ought to be done". For instance, those who take courses in homiletics invariably structure their messages in the way they have been taught. Consequently large numbers of people, all of whom have taken the same course, preach in exactly the same way (an illustration, three points and a conclusion). Not having been taught how I should preach, I have always felt free to do what the Lord leads me to do, whether or not it agrees with the conventional wisdom. People have liked this and I don't think it has ever been a drawback.

As the youth group grew it became clear that we needed to "do something" with them during the summer break. We decided to take them to Timothy Lake, a body of water situated in the Oregon Cascades. Several of the parents came along to cook and generally organize things. Both kids and adults had a great time hiking in the forest and messing about in the water.

On the evening of October 12th, 1962, Edna and I had gathered a large number of children in the church basement. We had planned a party for them. Suddenly the lights went out and we heard a roaring noise outside. This was the beginning of the famous "Columbus Day Wind Storm" that swept Oregon, Washington and parts of California. Authorities tell us that it was the most intense cyclone-type storm to hit the western states in recorded history. Eleven billion board feet of lumber were blown down and a number of lives lost as the result of it. We tried to keep control of the children but they began to exit in the darkness and disappear. Fortunately they lived close at hand and must have run straight home. We gathered those who were left and took them up to our house for shelter. The wind was so intense that it actually forced its way between the panes of glass and the wooden frame. Trees crashed down in all directions and debris blew violently across the road's surface. When the wind began to drop I decided to deliver the kids home in the car but discovered I had a flat. We jacked up the car but the wind blew it off again. Then some of the older boys helped brace the car against the wind and we succeeded in changing the wheel. It was a hazardous drive to the various homes. Trees lay across the roads in places and branches were flying like missiles but eventually I completed the delivery and was thankful to return to the house. Later we saw some of the damage that had been done further up in the mountains. Heavy rain had created raging streams that had rushed down from above, carrying trees and houses before it.

One of the things I lacked at Redland was an office. There was no office at the church and too many kids at home for me to study properly. The men of the church therefore decided to build me an office beside the house. First they poured a concrete floor and then erected a wooden "box" about twelve feet square. It was unheated and damp but at least it afforded a quiet place in which to study. As a lay preacher in England I could use messages several times because I visited a different church each Sunday. But as a resident pastor, the pace was more exacting. I preached Sunday mornings and evenings, taught the adult Sunday school class and ran the youth group after the evening service. Every meeting demanded a fresh message and I therefore needed adequate study time. The fact that I had not received the benefit of formal theological training made study even more important.

This was where I learned to rest in the Lord. He had placed us in this location and we believed He would supply our every need in order to carry on the ministry. Of course, the enemy was always on hand to tell me I couldn't do it, and he was right, of course. I could not do it in my own strength, but the Lord never let me down. Week by week He gave me my messages. He clarified the Scriptures for me and opened my eyes to the truth. I spent many hours delving into the Scriptures and reading commentaries. I shall always be grateful to Alan Redpath for his books, "Victorious Christian Living" and "Victorious Christian Service". They were expositions of Joshua and Nehemiah respectively that introduced me to the untold riches of the Old Testament. They opened my eyes to the way in which Old Testament events brilliantly illustrate New Testament teaching. Since those early days I have never forgotten this principle, nor wavered from preaching verse-by-verse through entire books of the Bible.

I learned another lesson during those early days that I remembered and practiced throughout the years of my ministry. This lesson was never to go to the commentaries until what the Holy Spirit had shown me personally had been written down on paper. The commentaries were then useful only to check the accuracy of what I had prepared. Messages based on other people's scholarship are second hand and dry. To be fresh, a message must come directly from God to the preacher through the Scriptures, not from commentaries. As somebody once remarked: "The Scriptures shed so much light on the commentaries!"

Early in our ministry God gave Edna and me the Scriptures we took as our life's verses. To Edna He gave Philippians 4:13:

> *"I can do all things through Christ who strengthens me."*

To me He gave Joshua 1:9:

> *"Have not I commanded you? Be strong and of a good courage;*
> *be not afraid, neither be thou dismayed, for the Lord your God is*
> *with you, whithersoever you go."*

119

As we learned to lead a congregation there were many times when those verses provided us with the strength we lacked. Through the years we faced challenges which we felt unqualified to meet. Our temptation was to judge our chances of solving them on the basis of our own lack of wisdom and strength. It was then that God's word gave us courage. It was not for us to solve the problem. It was our role to commit it totally to the Lord and allow Him to solve it in His own way. He always did.

Along the way, Edna started a nursery for the babies during the morning services. She felt it would encourage young couples to attend -- which it did. This was a novel idea to many of the older people but a welcome development for young mothers. The men of the church constructed a small room off the vestibule to house the nursery and some of the women helped look after the children. More and more young parents with children began to attend services.

During the Spring each year, Village Missions held a week-long conference at the Canon Beach Conference grounds. All VM pastors and their families were expected to attend. With great excitement we set out the first year for the conference. We had heard that Canon Beach was on the Pacific coast and in our ignorance we had mental images of palm trees and grass skirts. It was quite a revelation when we rounded the bend above Canon Beach and saw the grey stretches of ocean, bordered with pine forests. However, the conference itself was a great uplift, and we learned to love the Oregon coast, despite its cold breezes and gray skies. We were thrilled to sit under the ministry of truly great speakers, who fed us from the Word. They encouraged and inspired us to return to the field with a renewed vision. J. Sidlow Baxter, Vance Havner, J. Vernon McGee, Dr. M.R. DeHaan and many others took their turn at the center. It was at one of these conferences that we first met Dr. John Hunter, who became a dear friend and mentor in the years to come.

The Lord's Provision

Our income was extremely limited during those first days. The small wage the church was able to pay plus the additional support from the

Church of the Open Door came to a very small total. Had we been required to pay rent, there would probably have been insufficient for our needs, but the parsonage came as part of our support. One day, Edna and I drew money from the bank for housekeeping and went to buy the week's groceries. We then returned and paid some bills. However, I failed to first deduct the housekeeping from our balance, so that when we added everything up we were overdrawn by five dollars. That sum doesn't sound very much by today's standards but in 1962 it was significant. We had nowhere to turn for the money and we felt it would be a bad testimony for the local pastor to be overdrawn, so we took the matter to the Lord. We said, "Father, we didn't mean to overdraw. It was a genuine mistake. Could you please send us five dollars -- fairly soon?"

The very next day we received a letter from a lady in Milwaukee whom we had never met. It contained a five dollar bill and in the letter she wrote: "You don't know me but I heard of you through the church. I lost a five dollar bill and asked the Lord to help me find it. I found it in the pocket of a housecoat I don't remember wearing and the Lord told me to send it to you." The letter was postmarked two days before our need was created!

Edna writes: "As I look back on the Redland years, I am amazed at how God had been preparing me for this work throughout my life. My whole early upbringing involved watching my mother work and provide meals for a large family and create a happy haven for them. My father started his adult life as a soldier in the first world war and on his discharge carried on his life as a carpenter. After some years, he became the Workers' Representative at Huntley and Palmers biscuit factory (an extra unpaid position) because of his concern for others. The extra work kept him busy most evenings, so we children seldom saw him. Then came the war years, which taught me to live frugally, to make do with few clothes and luxuries. In our school days, our Home Economy classes were all about how to "make do and mend", how to stretch our meager rations as far as we could. "Budget" was a familiar word to me.

"Now God was teaching me, more than at any time in my life -- what He meant in Matthew 6:25-35: "*Therefore I say unto you, Take no thought for your life, what ye shall eat, or what ye shall drink; nor yet for your body, what ye shall put on. Is not the life more than meat, and the body than raiment? 26 Behold the fowls of the air: for they sow not, neither do they reap, nor gather into barns; yet your heavenly Father feedeth them. Are ye not much better than they? 27 Which of you by taking thought can add one cubit unto his stature? 28 And why take ye thought for raiment? Consider the lilies of the field, how they grow; they toil not, neither do they spin: 29 And yet I say unto you, That even Solomon in all his glory was not arrayed like one of these. 30 Wherefore, if God so clothe the grass of the field, which to day is, and to morrow is cast into the oven, shall he not much more clothe you, O ye of little faith? 31 Therefore take no thought, saying, What shall we eat? or, What shall we drink? or, Wherewithal shall we be clothed? 32 (For after all these things do the Gentiles seek:) for your heavenly Father knoweth that ye have need of all these things. 33 But seek ye first the kingdom of God, and his righteousness; and all these things shall be added unto you. 34 Take therefore no thought for the morrow: for the morrow shall take thought for the things of itself. Sufficient unto the day is the evil thereof."* The Lord was teaching us to walk by faith.

"What a thrilling time is was! But, of course Satan made sure there were times when we forgot for a moment and feared. Being so far from our loved ones meant we were drawn closer to God and to one another. A telephone call to England in those days cost $25 for five minutes - - out of the question on our budget! So our only communication was by letter, which took over a week to get to its destination. Having no family to go to we learned to take each need to the Lord. It deepened and humbled me to realize that the God of the universe knew our every need and graciously supplied.

"There was a couple who pastored a church in a small community close by. The husband was also the janitor at the school. They were not blessed with children of their own but Mrs. Reno loved to sew. Thanks to her, for the four years we were in Redland our girls had beautiful matching dresses each Easter. My sister, Olive, who lived in Wisconsin, also had four little girls and she often shared hand-me-downs with us.

"These four and a half years were such a challenge as well as a great blessing. In addition to caring for the six of us and the home, I was learning to be a pastor's wife. One of the things we were taught during our orientation at Stonecroft was that we should make no special friends among the people of the congregation. We were to be friends with all. Having left our whole family behind, this was an extra burden, different from being just a church member.

"One of our young girls became close to us and our family. Pat was our baby sitter and we were encouraged by her faithful attendance at church and her spiritual growth. Pat later went on to Multnomah School of the Bible. While there she met her husband, Ken, and they became Village Missionaries, where they continue to serve today."

In fact, Edna became (and continues to be) an outstanding pastor's wife. She is not one of those women who "run everything" and claim a prominent place in every activity. She prefers to work behind the scenes. Her skill lies in her ability to quietly minister to the women in the congregation, without regard to their education or social standing. She exercises a subtle but powerful influence in the church and has consistently won the love of every congregation we have served. Many testimonies point gratefully to the gentle advice she has given to individuals and groups through the years.

Life in the 1960s

One morning we glanced out of our living room window and saw flames rising as high as the trees from a neighbor's house and our neighbor crossing the road, still in her nightdress, carrying a baby and leading a toddler by the hand. She had sustained burns which Edna tried to sooth with cold water. The house, a small cabin, was badly damaged but she and her children had managed to escape. Evidently the little boy had played with the stove while his mother was still sleeping. Edna looked after the children while I drove their mother to the hospital in Oregon City. She recovered fairly quickly but the incident made a deep impression on the family. They started coming to church and after a few Sundays the couple walked down the aisle hand-in-hand to receive

Christ as their Savior. Sometimes it takes a frightening experience to shake us loose from our complacency.

On another occasion I was called to the bedside of an old man who was dying. He was not one of our church people but had indicated that he wanted to see a minister. He was very frail and unable to carry on a conversation. It was with great difficulty that he could say anything at all. As I stood beside him he made a sign that he wanted to say something to me. I bent down close to his mouth and he said just one word: "How?" I explained the way of salvation and asked him if he understood. He nodded. Then I asked him if he wished to receive Jesus Christ as his Savior. He nodded again. Within a short while he had died.

I was reminded of the parable Jesus told about the householder who hired laborers at various times of the day. Those who were hired at the eleventh hour received the same wages as those who had worked all day. The old man I had visited in the hospital trusted Christ at the eleventh hour but received the same salvation as those who were saved in their childhood. He had no time to enjoy it on this earth but he went to Heaven with the same forgiveness, the same life, the same inheritance that were offered to everyone. If he had Christ, he had it all!

I suppose most people who were alive in 1963 can remember where they were on November 22nd, when President Kennedy was assassinated. Edna was in the kitchen preparing a meal and I was up in the attic storing some belongings. Edna shouted up to me that they had just reported on the radio that someone had fired at the president as he and Jackie were driving through Dallas, Texas and that he was seriously injured. There followed the series of announcements concerning his condition and then finally it was confirmed that he had died of his wound. Lyndon Johnson was hastily sworn into office aboard Air Force One at Andrews Air force Base. The nation was thrown into gloom and anger toward the assassin. However, history is composed of dramatic events and God allowed the tragedy to take place for a reason known only to Him. At the time of his death, about 16,000

American "advisors" were in Vietnam, but the war had not officially begun. It began to escalate under President Johnson and soon grew into a major conflict.

It was during the 1960's that people started to give my name, "Ashley", to girls. For centuries prior to this it had been exclusively male. Later, in 1973, a television soap opera containing a female character named Ashley, added to its popularity as a girl's name. In America, by the end of the last century, "Ashley" had become so accepted as a girl's name that surprise bordering on disbelief was displayed when I revealed my name. I began to receive junk mail addressed to "Mrs. Ashley Day", "Ms. Ashley Day" or "Miss Ashley Day" and telemarketers make themselves even more annoying than usual by insisting that they want to speak to *"Ashley* Day", who obviously could not be me! Today "Ashley" is firmly established as a girl's name and I am looked upon as something of a curiosity. Our grandson, Ashley Brian, used his second name (Brian) during his high school years but toward the end of his service in Iraq he changed back to "Ashley" in defiance of the common fashion.

The sixties were the years of the "Hippie Movement". Beginning primarily as a youth movement it spread quickly through the colleges to adult groups. It was basically a revolution against the status quo. Hippies allowed their hair and beards to grow long, did not bother wash, indulged heavily in drugs, practiced sexual promiscuity and promoted psychedelic rock music. They were known as "Flower Children" because they enjoyed all things natural. They claimed to love everyone but behaved violently toward authority of any kind. They were in the forefront of demonstrations against the Vietnam war. During the time we lived in Redland they were very much in evidence -- not in Redland itself, which was too remote, but in Portland and other more heavily populated areas. I remember, later, driving our Volkswagen bus to Portland. A lone Hippie stood by the roadside thumbing a lift. Feeling pity for him I stopped to give him a lift and immediately several others jumped out of the bushes and piled in. We continued our journey with a full load and the windows open!

Building Program

By 1965, our congregation had grown considerably and we were becoming cramped in our little church. Toward the end of the year we began to plan a new building. It would join the rear of the existing church and extend back toward our house. It would be large enough to accommodate double the number of our present congregation and would include proper toilet facilities. It was far from an architect's design and the men of the church determined to build it themselves. Building permits were not yet enforced so there was nothing to slow progress except money and labor. Several men in the congregation had building experience and we had enough cash to begin the work. Eventually there came a day when the footings were marked out. Immediately we hit a problem. We were building on solid rock! There was no question of digging footings. blasting would be nearer the mark. However, little by little we carved out the necessary footings with hammer and chisel. It took a long time and sometimes there would be only one man banging away. Often that one man was me and the project seemed huge. However, eventually it was completed and ready for the concrete to be poured. The walls went up and the trusses were fixed in their place. Soon the roof and walls were sheathed with plywood and the building began to assume its final shape. There was quite a lot of excitement when we cut through the rear wall of the old building to gain access into the new. The facility seemed huge after our cramped quarters, though in reality is was very modest in size.

It was now five years since our last baby had been born and our desire for a boy to complete our family was still strong. We therefore asked the Lord to give us a boy but told Him we would be happy with either sex. The Lord answered our prayer and we soon became aware that baby number five was on the way. The arrival date was set for February, 1966. When the time came, Edna went into the Oregon City Hospital under the care of a very capable and compassionate doctor (Dr. Cleland). It was a small hospital but had a warm and personal atmosphere about it. The girls went to stay with one of the church families and I was instructed by the congregation to ring the church bell if the baby proved to be a boy. As with the other deliveries, the wait seemed endless (much longer for Edna than for me) but eventually the news was proclaimed. Andrew

Philip had arrived! Edna had suspected for some time that a boy was on the way because of the way he had kicked and wriggled during the last few months of her pregnancy. He was different from the girl babies in more ways than one. He was active from the outset and pushed up on his arms to look around as soon as we brought him home. It was late when I left the hospital but after driving home I rang the church bell with all my might. Next morning the whole valley knew we had a son and the news generated great excitement.

About the same time we received news that my grandmother had died, just short of her 102nd birthday. She was born Martha Mercy Hazeldine on January 29th, 1865. The Hazeldine family lived in Ramsgate, Kent., where they maintained a ship's chandler's business. Alyson was very impressed and reported to her teacher that her Great Grandmother had died at 201. When the teacher disbelieved her, she became quite indignant and demanded confirmation from us. She was disappointed when we were unable to oblige.

CHAPTER 8

Lookout, California

In the Autumn of 1966 a situation arose which eventuated in our leaving Redland. A family had joined us the previous year from a nearby town. They had a number of beautiful children and soon became a regular part of our fellowship. Everything was normal and they fitted in admirably. The children became members of the newly formed children's choir and the couple participated in the church activities. What we did not know was that the wife had been seriously abused in her younger days. This had left her with deep psychological problems. In time she became attracted to me and began to make embarrassing advances. I immediately informed Edna and we resolved to deal with the situation together. However, as time passed the problem intensified and we decided to call Mr. Duff for counsel. All we desired was some advice concerning how best to handle the situation. However, Mr. Duff listened in silence and then told me that he felt we should immediately move to another field. He instructed us to give our resignation the next day. This was far from what we expected or desired but reluctantly we did as we were bidden. The congregation (who had no idea what was going on) was stunned. They couldn't understand the reason for such a sudden decision and we did not feel free to inform them.

Mr. Duff called next day to tell us he was sending us to Howard, Colorado. He said it was a good field and the incumbent missionary had decided to move. With that information we began to pack our things ready to leave. Mercifully, the mission had it's own removal truck to transport existing missionaries between fields, so we had no need to sell the belongings we had accumulated during the past four years. When everything was ready for the removal truck, we received another call from Mr. Duff to say that the missionary in Howard had decided not to move after all. He arrived later that day and gave us a choice between two fields. One was in the deep south, near the Mexican border, and the other was in the high country of California. Neither sounded particularly attractive but we had to go somewhere and chose the field in California. Hot locations were not attractive to fair-skinned English people so California sounded the more favorable of the two.

The truck arrived on time and having loaded our belongings we set out on the journey to our new field. It was bewildering to leave Redland so suddenly but orders were orders. We assumed that the Lord had allowed it for a good reason.

Our route lay down Highway 5 to Weed. There we turned east toward Alturas and eventually climbed up to our new field. It was totally unlike Redland. Its name, "Lookout", suited it, due to its altitude (about 4750 ft). It was situated on a high plateau surrounded by even higher mountains and populated almost entirely by cattle ranchers. The town itself seemed almost derelict. Jenny commented as we drove through it: "Won't it be fun to live in a ghost town!" The truck led us across the valley until we arrived at a very nice brick rancher. This was to be our new home. The house was much larger and more modern than our previous parsonage. There were also some substantial items of furniture, making our few belongings appear less sparse. The kitchen was beautiful and there were plenty of bedrooms to accommodate the family. The owner met us graciously, showed us the property and then departed, leaving us to settle in and make ourselves comfortable.

The little church, just down the road from the house, was an ugly affair, with a square tower and a general air of neglect. One of the residents later commented that she thought it was "the prettiest little church she had ever seen", causing us to wonder where in the world she had been to draw her comparisons! The interior was cold and uninviting. On our first Sunday we faced a very small congregation, which seemed unresponsive and indifferent. It was quite a contrast to Redland.

Knowing that we had to bring in wood for the winter, Edna and I took our station wagon into the forest nearby and tried to saw some logs with a small bow saw, which was all we had. The results, of course, were pitiful. But we need not have worried because the owner of our house and some other men went up a short while later and cut down a huge dead tree, sawed it into slices with their chainsaws and filled our garage with the big rounds of wood. All I had to do was chop it into smaller chunks.

As the winter drew on, snow fell in great abundance. Huge icicles hung from the eves and almost reached the ground. The atmosphere was so cold that the air sparkled with a million little stars of frost and our breath froze on our noses. The wind carved out blue caves in the snow drifts and the trees wore a permanent coat of frost. It was then that we experienced the provision of the Lord. Coming as we had from western Oregon, where the climate was mild, we were unprepared for the bitter cold of the high country. We had no money to buy winter clothes and anticipated the winter with some anxiety. However, we need not have worried. Just before the cold hit we received a big barrel from the Church of the Open Door. It contained warm clothes for the children, so that when the cold weather arrived they were equipped and ready. When Edna first took the lid off the barrel she stood and cried because our house was so cold and there on the top of the contents were some little warm sleeper suits for Andy. The folks in Milwaukee must have done their homework and recognized we were in for temperatures much lower than we had experienced before.

A similar demonstration of the Lord's care came at Christmas time. Nicky announced one day that what she desired most for Christmas was a "Raggedy Ann" doll. She had been reading a book about it in school. The problem was that we had already purchased her present and had neither the time nor the money to meet her request. We told her to pray about it. Maybe the Lord would provide. God already knew our needs because just before Christmas, a parcel arrived from a friend in Redland. Inside were four Raggedy Ann dolls and a Raggedy Andy for Andy! In neither case had we communicated with the people who so generously remembered us but the Lord knew both our needs and our "wants" and fulfilled them in such a way as to bring glory to Himself. These instances of God's provision provided practical teaching for the children that none of them has ever forgotten.

During that winter our power was cut off for quite a long period. We kept warm by keeping the wood fire burning and melting snow to provide water. However, these harsh conditions eventually came to an end. Winter gave way to the Spring, the deep snow melted and we were able to move around more easily. The wet ground gradually dried and gave way to dust, so that cars kicked up large clouds as they drove along the roads.

As winter drew to a close, Andy, then about nine months old, fell sick with pneumonia. The local doctor and his nurse were both German and spoke German to one another in the presence of their patients. This made us feel very uncomfortable. We had nothing against the doctor but having come through the war years in England, we involuntarily connected the German language with the enemy. The next nearest doctor was in Burney, about eighty miles away over the mountain. We therefore drove this road several times until Andy recovered.

When Spring arrived, the kids were intrigued to watch the cattle brought in from the hills and the calves roped and branded. It was a real-life "wild west" atmosphere. School in Adin, a small community nearby, was an unhappy experience for them, however. The kids there were rough and did not react well to outsiders coming into their territory. This was a feeling we all experienced. We were able to do general pastoral work. We held Sunday services, visited in the community, attended local functions and generally reached out to the people. We did succeed in starting a Sunday evening fellowship in our home, which a fair number of people supported, but nothing else seemed to work very well. It was a dry time in our ministry. I attempted to reach out to the owner of our house by helping with chores on his farm but never succeeded in making much progress.

To make matters worse, unlike Redland, Lookout was not self-supporting financially. This meant that the small income we had received in Oregon was reduced drastically. Mission policy was that if the field was able to support itself with offerings, the money pledged to the missionary by supporting churches or individuals was paid directly to him. However, if the field was not self-supporting, support from donors was used to make up the basic amount. This created hardship on the part of the missionary in a non-self-supported field like Lookout. To add to the agony, we received letters periodically from the home office urging us to raise the field to self-supporting status. This could be done only by greatly increasing the number of attendees willing to give of their substance. The general character of Lookout and its sparse inhabitants made this task almost impossible.

CHAPTER 9

Rockaway, Oregon

Angered by the letters from headquarters and discouraged by the work, I eventually wrote to Mr. Duff. Perhaps if I had been more mature at the time I would have quietly accepted the situation and trusted the Lord to work things out. As it was, I wrote complaining that he had "sent us to a derelict field and then threatened to have a heart attack when we didn't have it self-supporting in the first six months!" Three days later Mr. Duff stood on our doorstep. He had driven all the way from Dallas, Oregon, in response to my letter. He told us he recognized the situation in which he had placed us and was prepared to do something about it. Sitting down with a map, he told us about a string of small communities along the Oregon coast that needed a pastor. The name of the main community was Rockaway. It was situated about twenty-five miles south of Cannon Beach. If we were interested, he would arrange for us to candidate there. We told him we were very interested and after a night's "rest" on the couch in our living room he drove back to Dallas.

A letter soon arrived from Rockaway, inviting us to visit and setting a proposed date. It was with a strong sense of anticipation that we packed the children into the car a few days later and headed for the Oregon coast. Like all its neighbors up and down the western seaboard, Rockaway had a battered, windswept appearance. The buildings all seemed to be sand-blasted and some leaned as if pushed over by the wind. The constant roar of the sea formed a background to every conversation but the air was exhilarating and the people extremely friendly. We were received graciously and the congregation responded beautifully to the message on Sunday morning. Following the service, I was interviewed at some length by the board. This was a new experience for me. After Redland and Lookout, neither of which had visible organization, the idea of pastoring a church that actually had a board was somewhat intimidating. However, I survived and the following morning we headed back to California.

The next few days were spent praying and waiting. Would the folks in Rockaway accept us or would Mr. Duff have to try to find somewhere different? Only time would tell and that seemed to drag by very slowly. Eventually the letter we were awaiting arrived and we were almost afraid to open it. However, our fears were unfounded. With great excitement we read that I had been officially called to pastor the Rockaway Community Church. It was with a sense of profound relief and gratitude to the Lord that we began to pack our belongings once again. Suspicion from the field persisted to the end. When the truck arrived, a few days later, the owner's sister came and sat in our living room to make sure we took nothing belonging to them. We had no regrets about leaving Lookout but sensed a thrill of anticipation as we contemplated beginning a new ministry in Rockaway.

The first official function in Rockaway took place seven days after our arrival, when the women threw a party to honor Andy's first birthday. He was personally not particularly impressed (though he enjoyed the cake) but we were grateful for their kindness. This warm atmosphere continued throughout our six-and-a-half years there. Rockaway was a wonderful place in which the kids could spend their growing up years. In 1967 the girls' ages were 14, 11, 9 and 7 years respectively and Andy was just twelve months old. They therefore spent their most impressionable years with the free run of a wide expanse of beach bordered by sand dunes, in which they played continually. Andy was too young to keep up with their activities in his own strength, so his sisters trundled him round in a push chair wherever they went. He was always part of the gang.

Accommodation

Our first home in Rockaway was only temporary. It was a small house bordering Highway 101, with a big attic bedroom upstairs, where the girls slept, and a small bedroom on the ground floor which Edna, Andy and I used. The interesting thing about this house was its proximity to the railroad. A line runs down the coast beside Highway 101. In Rockaway it borders on the main street itself. Our front door was perhaps twenty feet to the west of the line, so that when a train crawled past, sounding its horn loudly, our windows were completely blocked by its bulk. It seemed almost to run through the house. The building shook as if an earthquake had struck and each set of wheels would "chonk" over the joints in the rails, as if someone were beating an anvil with an immensely heavy hammer. It was quite an experience and the children eagerly looked forward to the next train.

Fortunately, we did not live in our first house very long. The church board diligently sought a new home for us, being mindful of the size of our family. Some weeks after our arrival they settled on a house on the east side of highway 101, secluded from the traffic and much further from the railroad tracks. It was a comfortable home with accommodation for all our needs. Andy and we had bedrooms on the ground floor, while the girls had rooms above. One unusual characteristic was that the downstairs toilet was supported by an upright log under the floor. If we happened to be sitting there when a train passed on the other side of highway 101, the toilet swayed noticeably. We became used to this phenomenon but visitors were startled if they happened to enthroned when a train came through. They assumed we were having an earthquake. Across the street from the house was an old detached building used as a garage. It had an attic above, approached by a ladder. The girls thought this was great fun and immediately commandeered it as their playhouse. They spent many happy hours playing there.

Rockaway enabled us to grow in both our faith and pastoral experience. It was different in every way from Lookout and we soon grew to love the people. Even now, after forty years, we still count some of them as friends. Life became very busy in Rockaway. In the beginning, I preached twice on Sundays, taught the adult Sunday school class, directed the choir, taught the Wednesday evening Bible study, and ran the youth group. In between, I conducted weddings and funerals, counseled those in need and visited in the area. As I look back, I wonder how I managed to keep up this pace, but "you do what you have to do" and the Lord gave me the strength. As time passed He raised up helpers and the load became lighter. Nevertheless, it remained a very busy ministry and I think my family suffered because of it. We managed to support the kids by attending most events at their schools but demands of the pastorate robbed them of the attention they might have received otherwise. This is a problem with any public service. Father always seems to be looking after other people's needs while the family is at least partially neglected. Mercifully, the children remained happy. They seemed not to resent the demands made upon me by the ministry.

One of the ground rules set by Village Missions was that a pastor had to serve for five years before he was eligible for ordination. Now that this initial period had been fulfilled, plans for my ordination were set in motion. I prepared my doctrinal statement and in June, 1967, just five years after our arrival in Redland, I was examined by an ordination council at the Canon Beach Conference Center and later ordained in the chapel there. I felt I was now officially confirmed in the work God had called me to do.

Activities

After a while, the youth group grew in size and we felt we wanted to do something special with them. Up on Mount Hood, there is a trail at the 6,000 to 8,000 feet level, that encircles the mountain. It is about fifty miles in length. We suggested that we take the youth group up there and spend a week hiking this trail. Our suggestion was enthusiastically approved by the kids and we began preparations. Nobody at that time was properly equipped but we agreed to go and see how we got on. I made everybody a wooden frame for their packs, using 1-inch dowels and canvas webbing but they were far inferior to the real thing and proved very uncomfortable. After driving to Timberline Lodge, we left the cars in the parking lot and set out along the Timberline Trail. It was great fun but we soon discovered that our lack of adequate equipment made the task much more difficult than it should have been. After a couple of days, we decided to retrace our steps, but we were still enthusiastic about the project and determined to try again the following year.

When the next Summer arrived, we made better preparations. Back-packs, boots, sleeping bags, rain gear, freeze-dried food and tube tents were all purchased. We looked more like a group of explorers preparing to tackle Kilimanjaro than high schoolers hiking the Timberline Trail. However, it was a big challenge to us and we set off in high spirits - - Edna and I plus seventeen high school students. As before, we left our cars in the parking lot at Timberline Lodge and set off along the trail. This time we found progress much easier, though the trail was a challenge. Instead of running level, it seemed to take us either straight up or straight down. This made progress slow and some of the kids found it tough going. We made it a rule that the group must stay with the slowest member. This was observed good-naturedly and none was left behind.

As we climbed above the tree line some nasty weather blew in and we donned our rain gear. We looked rather like a group of futuristic camels, with our capes draped over our backpacks. Toward nightfall, we came across a small empty cabin belonging to the Park Service. It was there to provide shelter for passing hikers. We piled in, grateful for a dry place to spend the night and made ourselves as comfortable as possible. It was a tight squeeze but the kids enjoyed the experience. They gained valuable experience trying to get a fire going in the rain. Next morning, the weather had cleared and we were able to press on along the trail without the hindrance of our rain capes.

The remainder of the week was warm and dry. The high alpine meadows were ablaze with flowers and the scenery was outstanding. Each evening we had a devotional time and nights were spent in clearings along the way. Our tube tents worked well, except that the wind kept changing direction during the night. We would pitch our tents at an angle away from the wind in the evening but invariably it would be blowing right in on us by morning. There were plenty of fresh mountain springs to provide water and our freeze-dried food provided nourishment, although the altitude made it take a long time to cook. At the end of the week we trudged back to Timberline Lodge, having circumvented the mountain, crossed glaciers and snow fields and climbed thousands of feet of rocky trail. We were weary but happy. Further down the mountain we celebrated at Government Camp, by crowding into the Huckleberry Inn and eating huge cinnamon rolls. It had been a profitable time.

Canon Beach

Several interesting opportunities presented themselves during our time in Rockaway. Often I was called by the Conference Center at Canon Beach to lead the singing. Of course, we were still in the "hymn book era" at that time and I conducted conventional services for the various speakers. I worked regularly with John Hunter, who had become a close friend, and the conference center called me whenever there was a gap in their schedule. On one occasion the advertised speaker was suddenly taken ill and I had to fill in without notice. Another time I led the music for Dr. J. Vernon McGee. He was somewhat gruff in his manner and didn't particularly enjoy the singing part of the services. One evening, as I announced a hymn, he stood up and said loudly, "We don't need any more hymns. Let's get on with it!" With that he mounted the platform and began to teach. We enjoyed his ministry. One evening he opened his message by first inviting us to turn to a passage in Romans. Then he said, "I have studied Romans for many years. I have preached from it in the church and on the radio and have written books on it. But when I get to Heaven I'm going ask the apostle Paul what Romans is all about!"

As the youth group developed in Rockaway, some members were able to lead the singing with guitars. One day, during casual conversation at our couples meeting, I mentioned that it would be fun if we could get hold of an old beaten-up string bass that I could play with the kids. A week or so later, when we arrived for our meeting, the couples all seemed to have grins on their faces. We entered the living room and there stood a beautiful (not beaten-up) bass. They had clubbed together and purchased it for me. Now I had to learn to play it! I worked hard at this and soon I was able to provide the base line for our singing. Eventually we became quite proficient and were even invited to sing at meetings in neighboring communities. We named the instrument "Elijah" because he came out of nowhere to bring fire into the youth group! Elijah still stands in our home, an honored guest.

The witness of children

It is striking to see how powerful the witness of children can be in a family. In our Sunday school were a brother and sister who attended regularly. Their parents believed it was good for them to attend church but they (the parents) felt no need to do so themselves. Their father was a sheriff's deputy and their mother also worked locally. The children often asked their parents to accompany them to church, without success. But they refused to give up. One Easter morning the parents finally consented.

As is always the case on Easter morning, the way of salvation was clearly given, and although it produced no visible response at the time, the Lord was evidently at work. Next week, the father (Lyle) visited me in my office -- something he had never done before. He was in uniform, with guns and mace and handcuffs dangling from his belt, which produced an intriguing squeaky noise when he moved. His avowed reason for visiting me was to give a donation to the church but I sensed from his manner that there was a deeper reason beneath the surface.

After a while, as we talked together, Lyle indicated his desire to receive Christ as his Savior and I had the joy of praying with him. Before leaving, he suggested that I might like to visit his house to speak to his wife (Darlene) and the next day I did so. She was completely ready and prayed to receive Christ in such a matter-of-fact manner that I wondered if she had fully understood. I went through the way of salvation a second time but there was no doubt about her understanding or sincerity. As the direct result of the children's witness, the whole immediate family was now united in the Lord. Through their testimony, members of the extended family later received Christ. Eventually, Lyle and Darlene left their jobs in Rockaway and volunteered to serve full time with the mission, a task they fulfilled to the highest standard. In recent years Lyle earned a degree in theology, thus crowning many years of faithful service for the Lord. The children, now married with families of their own, remain faithful to their original commitment.

Among our congregation was an elderly gentleman who was the embodiment of what an Old Testament prophet might have looked like. He had strong, finely cut features and white hair that tended to be unruly. He was outspoken and strong in his faith. His blue eyes were clear and his bearing commanded respect. Despite his powerful presence he possessed an uncanny ability to win the confidence of wild creatures. He had a special place up in the forest where he would sit for hours. Animals would approach him, so that he could actually touch them and speak to them and they seemed to be quite unafraid.

One day this "prophet" was having his hair cut at the local barber's shop. The barber gave him a bad time about his faith and professed that he (the barber) did not believe in the existence of God. He and other clients made fun of the "prophet" because he did. After his haircut was complete, the "prophet" fixed his bright blue eyes on the barber and said, "I am going home now and I'm going to ask God to strike you dead!" The barber was visibly shaken and the color drained from his face. "Hold on, now", he said, "there's no need to be like that." The "prophet" paused for a moment with his hand on the door knob and then replied, "What are you worried about? You don't believe there is a God, do you?" A silence had fallen over the shop as he left!

The Lord's faithful provision

Throughout our years of ministry we have been aware of the way in which the Lord has watched over us. Even in the smallest ways, which on the surface may seem mundane and unspectacular, we have been conscious of His loving care. Edna writes, "As I look back over my life I can recognize in seemingly small incidences the amazing love and kindness of our all-knowing God. That the God who created this whole universe should care about the needs (and even the wants) of my family always overwhelms me.

"There was a day in Rockaway, when Ashley was called away just at a time when I needed him. I felt my need was as important as the caller's and became angry. That day we had a group of fellow missionaries coming to our home for a day of prayer. It was a Monday and the older children had left for school. The house was messy after the weekend. All the rooms would be used because we would split into groups for prayer. Also I had needed Ashley to pick up Kool-Aid at the store for the children. As I worked to make the house presentable, the Holy Spirit convicted me and I asked for forgiveness for my anger. "Have I not promised to provide for your needs?" the still small voice reminded me.

"My chores finished, a car arrived and the first missionary walked through the door carrying a whole crate of milk! I was truly humbled and ashamed of my small faith. Apparently the milkman's truck had broken down and he had given the milk to our friends. Not only does the Lord supply our needs but I believe He sometimes delights in surprising us by giving us our wants as well.

"When Andy was a baby, I liked to dress him in the kind of clothes English babies wear. This was not easy because they were expensive and difficult to find. In any case, most of our clothing as Village Missionaries were "hand-me-downs". One day, as I walked into my favorite thrift store, the assistant said, "I have something I think you will like". She then laid out on the counter some beautiful soft knitted romper suits, just like English babies used. Needless to say, I was delighted. I guess only the Lord (and maybe someone from our own country) would understand my surprise and pleasure."

Soon after we went to live in Rockaway, the local grocery store was purchased by a man named Fred May. He was a "mover and shaker" and we soon felt the family's presence in the church. At the Christmas service in 1969, after the choir had sung one of John Peterson's cantatas, I closed the meeting but the people remained in their seats. Then Fred got up and announced that the church was going to send us back to England for a visit. This was a wonderful surprise. It would be the first time we had been home since our immigration, eleven years previously. Our parents had never seen Jill or Andy, who were now ten and four years old respectively. It was therefore a most exciting gift.

Much progress had been made in air travel since our original flight to the States. This time we flew from Seattle, over the north pole to London in a jet, a much quicker and less exhausting journey. While there, we were able to celebrate my parents' fiftieth anniversary and my sister's twenty-fifth. It was a great time of reunion which tended to lessen the sense of isolation we had felt, being so far from home. We returned to Rockaway refreshed and ready to get on with our ministry.

Radio Ministry

Fred May was also responsible for the beginning of our radio ministry. I had been invited by a radio station in Tillamook to present a week of morning devotions on the air. It was a courtesy they extended to all the local clergy on a rotation basis. This went off very well and Fred offered to sponsor a paid-for program, advertising his grocery store. This seemed to be a good opportunity and I asked the station if they would air a daily five-minute meditation. They agreed and the program "Think on This" was launched. The program consisted of devotions based upon everyday happenings that illustrated Biblical truth. We had no recording equipment and I had to visit the station each week to record the programs in their studio. "Think on This" was an immediate success. People all over the area tuned in each morning and we began to see new faces in church as the result. Once I received a speeding ticket and the local judge was disappointed when I paid it without contest because she had planned to have me share a "Think on This" message in the courtroom in place of a fine!

It was a daunting experience to sit down before a microphone for the first time. A glass panel separated me from the engineer and he told me "When the red light comes on, start speaking!" I sat there perspiring, my eyes fixed on the light, while he dealt with some advertisements. Then suddenly the red light glowed and I was "on"! I took a deep breath and began. The microphone showed no sign of emotion and the engineer was not much better, but I tried to imagine a small group of people listening and gradually my heart slowed down a little and I was able to breathe more normally. By the end of the broadcast my nervousness had almost disappeared.

In time, a radio station in Salem asked if they could carry the program, which extended the listening area enormously. The owner of the station was very encouraging and gave me one of his own microphones, enabling me to record the programs in the church office instead of driving into Tillamook. Our first tape recorder and the acoustics of the office were not of professional quality (I fashioned my first microphone stand out of coat hangers). Consequently, our initial programs were not up to the standard we would have liked them to be, but we did our best and the Lord honored our efforts.

After some time, I felt dissatisfied with being limited to the five-minute devotionals. I wanted to share God's Word on a deeper level. We therefore added a 30-minute expositional program, which we called "The Bible Says". This once-weekly program enabled me to teach through books of the Bible as I did in church and it was well received. However, not every listener appreciated it.

One day, as I worked in my office, a young lady knocked on the door. She was well dressed and had an intelligent, decisive manner. I assumed she wanted to see me about something concerning the church but upon taking the seat I offered her she said, "I have come to complain about your radio program. You have consistently, publicly insulted us and demeaned us, and I am here to warn you that unless you desist I will have your program removed from the air. My husband is the station owner!" I was speechless. I had no idea what had upset her. Then she revealed that she, her husband and most of the station staff were Jewish and they took exception to the passage in Romans that I was currently teaching. She told me I couldn't get away with it because she and her friends listened regularly and they had heard every word I had said.

At the time I was teaching in Romans 10, which speaks of the fact that the Jews of Paul's day had a zeal for God but not according to knowledge; that they, being ignorant of God's righteousness and going about to establish their own righteousness, had not submitted themselves to the righteousness of God. As I spoke about the Jews that persecuted Paul, my visitor and her friends thought I was spreading anti-Semitic propaganda. Fortunately, she allowed me to explain at some length what our study was really about, that we were not anti-Semitic but that this was simply what the Word of God said. We parted amicably and in fact, Edna and I were later invited to visit them in their home, which we counted as a privilege. Ever since then I have been careful to avoid giving the impression that today's Jews are being singled out for abuse when this and other passages like it are taught.

Unusual Marriage

I was approached one day by a couple who wished to be married. There was nothing unusual about this request but the couple making it were rather noteworthy. The bride to be (Chris) was a doctor's daughter and her fiancé (Steve) was clearly a Hippie. The odd mixture was not a reason for refusing to marry them and so the wedding was planned. When the day arrived, the scene in the church was quite striking. On the bride's side was a group of people dressed in traditional wedding clothes -- dresses, suits, ties etc -- while on the bridegroom's side sat a group of really ragged Hippies. The aisle between them acted as a great gulf, across which neither party dared to cross.

Although communication between the two groups was minimal, Edna and I did our best to not notice the contrast. We gave them all the same attention and attempted to make both parties feel comfortable. Eventually the festivities ground to a close and everyone went home. We assumed that to be the end of the matter and put it down to experience. However, next day when the morning service began, we were surprised to find a whole row of Hippies in the congregation. Our people were wonderful. They welcomed them and loved them, without taking any notice of their long hair, ragged clothes or smell of patuli oil. The next Sunday they were there again, and the next.

One Sunday, as the service was nearing an end, Edna glanced over to where our friends were sitting. One of them had his head bowed and big tears were running down his cheek. Soon afterwards, without anything having been said, they cut their hair, cleaned themselves up and could no longer be described as Hippies. Chris, Steve and several of their friends trusted Christ as their Savior and we rejoiced once again over the manifold grace of God. We conducted a Bible study group for them and saw them grow in their faith. Some time later there was a knock at the door and Steve stood there holding a beautiful big salmon. He told Edna he had prayed that day that God would give him a good one so he could pass it on to us, and God had answered his prayer! I am still not totally convinced of the legality of the catch but since the fish was already dead we accepted it in good faith.

Growing Problems

As well as taking God's Word to the community, our radio program brought our church to people's attention. It grew considerably as the result. Soon our little building became inadequate and we sought a solution. We provided a temporary fix by turning the seating round to face in the opposite direction and opening the room at the rear of the sanctuary to become part of the worship center. This provided much-needed additional seating but also created some initial difficulties. People had been used to entering the building through the front door, which was now behind the pulpit. On one occasion, the front door was left unlocked. A couple arrived late for the service, used the unlocked door, pulled aside the curtain that now concealed the doorway and stepped out onto the platform. They were embarrassed to find themselves confronting the whole congregation.

The shack

The back-to-front project solved our problem temporarily but before long it was obvious that something much more permanent had to be done. We looked around for land but were unable to find anything suitable. The land we really wanted was not for sale. It was a five or six acre piece owned by an old single man who lived in a tumbledown shack on the property. He did not attend the church but I had visited him several times and had a good relationship with him. One day I went to see him and explained the problem facing the church. I asked him if he might be interested in selling us his land, but he said he would not and we dropped the matter there. However, a day or so later he contacted the elders and said he would give the land to the church if we would exchange houses with him. That meant Edna, the children and I would have to leave our comfortable home and move into his old shack! The idea seemed unreal but the offer was too good to turn down. After praying about it, we agreed to make the exchange and there soon came a day when the idea became a reality. The church inherited the land, the old man inherited our house and we inherited his shack!

The shack had been occupied by the owner for over fifty years. It seemed to lean as if weary. A porch, approached by a flight of rickety steps, gave access to the front door. Very little house cleaning had been done through the years. The unpainted walls were made of wooden boards that had become dark with age, and the house smelled of old man and wood smoke. Members of the congregation turned out to help us clean. We scrubbed and washed until eventually it was deemed sufficiently sanitary for our family to occupy. There was not a lot of room for seven of us but we managed to squeeze in. The kids thought it was great fun. Nicky found an old drum in the shed and amused herself banging it in time with her singing.

The boat

During this time we decided to buy a boat. We ordered an aluminum row boat from Sears Roebuck and waited eagerly for its arrival. It was too big for Sears to deliver and so we drove to Tillamook in our Volkswagen bus to pick it up. We brought it home amid great excitement, tied to the roof of the bus. We had to stop along the way because the wind had blown it askew. Of course, *everyone* had to get out to fix the boat and in the process the dog escaped. He found the smells in this unfamiliar stretch of road very attractive and we had to chase him up and down for some time in order to bring him back.

A day or so later I thought I would give the girls a demonstration in the art of rowing, so we drove to the Nehalem river with our boat on the roof. The launching process was well organized, with each member drilled in the part she would play. We must have looked rather like a coastguard drill team as we lowered the boat from its perch and smartly carried it to the water. An onlooker exhibited a surprised look as the kids, duly decked out with new life jackets, performed their "duties".

Having all climbed aboard, I explained that we would first row upstream, against the current, so that when we were tired we could relax and allow the flow to carry us back. The girls were very impressed by my logic. The Nehalem river has quite a strong current and rowing was hard work. However, we kept going, grateful for the knowledge that when we had expended all our energy we would be able to drift back with leisure.

After some time of rowing we figured we had gone far enough and turned the boat round, expecting to feel the current begin to carry us back toward home. Instead, to our dismay we continued to move slowly upstream. We realized with horror that the tide had turned and the ocean was pushing its way up the river. There was nothing for it but to begin rowing again, only this time against the power of the ocean!

A very weary group eventually staggered into the house. It was very late, supper was spoiling and Edna was beginning to worry lest we had all been drowned. The boat lost its attraction after that and was eventually sent back to Sears for a refund.

Spiritual battle

We had our share of spiritual battles also. Late one Saturday evening, as I worked in my office at the church, going over my message for the following day, I experienced a spiritual struggle that shook me to my roots. The Lord spoke to me. I did not hear an audible voice but the message could not have been clearer even if I had heard it with my ears. He said, "I want you to give Andy to me!" Andy? How could I give him away - even to the Lord? He was then about five years old and precious to us. But the voice persisted: "I want you to give Andy to me!" My stomach seemed to be tied into knots. I prayed and pleaded and wept, fully believing that the Lord intended to take him away. I could not bring myself to release him. The whole idea seemed unreal. But the battle was lost before it began and eventually, in a flood of tears, I surrendered Andy into the Lord's hands. Despite the turmoil the struggle had produced, a strange peace came over me. I was able to function normally again and finish the work I had been doing. I think I knew something of what Abraham experienced when God asked him to sacrifice his only son. Of course, God had no intention of taking Isaac away and neither did He intend to take Andy. The struggle was in the giving, not in the taking. He wanted to see if I would make the sacrifice. Actually, He already knew the answer. He just wanted me to see it. At this writing, Andy is in his forties and has been in Christian service for about 15 years.

About this time, Jennifer left us for Capernwray Bible School in the north of England. It was hard to see her leave but she was excited to be going and we agreed that Capernwray was the best possible choice for her to make. We drove her to the airport and saw her off on her journey. She seemed vulnerable to us as she boarded the plane and prepared to take her flight across the Atlantic alone. Back in the car, Andy said, "Look what I've found", and held up Jennifer's purse. It contained the money she had exchanged into English currency for her trip! Fortunately, friends had arranged to meet her at Heathrow and we knew they would take care of her.

New Building

Once back in Rockaway, our thoughts were again occupied with our new building. The land was now ours. Our next assignment was to move ahead with the project. There was a builder in the congregation named Dexter Job who willingly agreed to be our general contractor. A church in another part of the state was willing to allow us to use their blueprints, funds began to come in and arrangements were made to begin construction. With the exception of the excavating, concrete and crane to handle the big preformed beams, all labor was supplied from the congregation. We built the forms, poured the concrete, constructed the floor and ordered the big preformed laminated beams, which would form the shape of the building without the use of supporting pillars.

The problem was that we did not have the money to pay for the beams. They were expensive, but we ordered them in faith and then called a series of prayer meetings to ask God to provide the funds. We believed God had approved the project and He would give us the money to complete it. As the days passed and the delivery date drew closer, we became more and more anxious. We prayed earnestly that God would meet our need. Then one evening something remarkable happened. Instead of praying about the beams, people spontaneously began to confess sin and to seek forgiveness. In fact, we left the meeting that night without even mentioning the beams or the money to pay for them. It was a very sweet time and the Lord seemed to be very near. Needless to say, by the time the beams were delivered we had sufficient funds to pay for them. It was nothing to God to provide the money. He was much more interested in the hearts of the people than in their imagined need.

A crane arrived to raise the beams into their places and the real task of building began. Walls were erected, the tongue-and-groove boarding for the roof was hammered into place, plywood and siding were applied to the outside, while insulation and sheetrock were installed within. Men, women and children, all under the direction of our faithful builder, worked happily together throughout the period. A local stone mason volunteered to build a beautiful wall behind the platform. The stone was retrieved from quarries over a wide area. Our mason personally specified which quarries to visit, according to the color of the stone found in each. Carpet was laid, pews purchased from a church in Portland were installed, painting was completed and we were ready to move in. A large crowd gathered for the first service and filled the new sanctuary. They didn't all come back but our regular number continued to increase. God was blessing and there was great rejoicing.

Sadly, one of the first services I conducted in the new church was the funeral service for the toddler son of one of our prominent families. He had been playing in the yard of their home and had fallen into the lake. All efforts to revive him failed. Despite the sadness and the useless self-recriminations, the incident made a deep impression on the father. His spiritual life deepened considerably and in later years, after his retirement, he threw himself whole-heartedly into missionary work.

CHAPTER 10

Stonecroft, Kansas City, Missouri

Soon after the completion of our new building we received a visit from the leaders of our mission. They sat and talked with us for a while and then asked if I would be willing to accept the post of chaplain at the headquarters campus in Kansas City, Missouri. My task would be primarily to minister to the staff there. This invitation came as a surprise. We had just completed our new church building and the work was expanding healthily. In addition, the radio work was progressing nicely and it seemed to be a strange time to leave. However, we were asked to pray about it and give Mrs. Baugh and Miss Clark our answer. As we prayed and discussed the matter together, Edna and I felt the Lord was giving us the go ahead, and the following day we accepted the invitation.

When we submitted our resignation at the church meeting, the people were not very pleased. Understandably, I think they felt resentment toward the mission for coming in and taking their pastor from them. To make matters worse, unknown to us two other families had volunteered to work at Stonecroft, so that a total of twelve people from the congregation were preparing to leave. Mr. Duff had a pastor ready to take my place, which increased the feeling that this was a "railroad job". The people voiced their concern and though I did my best to calm their fears, it left a bad taste. Some who had been very supportive throughout our ministry cooled off and we sensed a reserve that had not been there before.

Just before we left for Kansas City, Edna received news that her mother had died. She was very fond of her mother and this came as a nasty blow.

153

Mum Kersley was a small, neat, compassionate lady, always ready to fill a need. She had an acute sense of humor and loved to laugh. She was artistic by nature, sensitive to beautiful things. In her younger days she enjoyed singing and took Edna along with her when she was booked to sing a solo. Edna would have liked to attend her mum's funeral but that was not possible. It was therefore with much sadness that we set off on our next adventure.

Once again, the mission truck was sent to Rockaway, our furniture and effects were loaded up and we set out on our way to Missouri. Moves like this are often hardest on the kids. The girls were deeply involved in their school and were at the age when the more exciting school activities were taking place. It was therefore not a good time to pull them away and take them from all their friends. They did not complain but we felt their sadness and that hurt us.

Stonecroft

Stonecroft had grown since our first visit there. Luxurious new buildings had been erected to provide accommodation and meeting rooms for the mushrooming staff, most of which was comprised of single ladies. We, however, were given an apartment in an older block, where we could enjoy greater privacy and freedom for the family. Pets were prohibited on campus but we had a small French Poodle, named Benjamin, which we had no intention of leaving behind. We therefore took him along and smuggled him in before anyone noticed. When news got out that Benjy had accompanied us, disapproval was expressed but by that time there was not much anyone could do about it. Benjy thus became a permanent resident.

The mission complex was like a miniature city. Apart from the private apartments, there was a dining room, in which we were expected to eat fairly frequently, and the kitchen where the meals were prepared. A large typing pool filled the main office in the admin building, a printing department, housing two or three big commercial printers, occupied the basement, a very large mailing department was housed in a separate building, and private offices for senior staff were tucked into various corners and annexes. A whole room was set aside for the computer, which resembled a row of refrigerators with reels that flicked to and fro. The room had to be kept as dust-proof as possible and at a set temperature. The total memory of this huge installation was less than that of the average laptop today. I was assigned an office (or rather a place where an office would be). Workmen were brought in to do the necessary construction and before long I was safely lodged in my own space, with an adjoining room dedicated to the production of radio programs. A friend of the mission, who was the owner of a prominent radio station in Kansas City, was coaxed into providing me with a professional mixing panel plus an agreement to air "Think on This" from his station. I set about the task of writing a new program every day. This was necessary in order to meet the demand.

It is an unfortunate truth that Christian organizations often look better from a distance that they do close up. Stonecroft was no exception. It was an establishment run by women for women and I soon found myself frustrated. There is no doubt that the Lord blessed the ministry but there was a "prissiness" about the organization that rendered it difficult for a man to accept. Edna tells me I am a rebel, which is probably true. I felt stifled by the rules and regulations that were imposed upon the staff. I also felt unfulfilled. I had been appointed ostensibly to take care of the spiritual needs of the workers but it soon became apparent that Mrs. Baugh and Miss Clark were in charge of that and I was there to do their bidding. I preached in the chapel, sat on the Stonecroft board, wrote and recorded radio programs and did my best to minister to the women but I was never free to function as I had anticipated.

Services in the chapel at Stonecroft were held during the week. This freed the staff to attend worship in local churches on Sundays. First, we tried a huge Southern Baptist church in Kansas City, where we found that men and women attended separate Sunday School classes. Edna was whisked off to a separate class, which didn't please us. The service was more like a concert than worship, so we decided to try another church. Many of the Stonecroft folks attended Colonial Presbyterian Church. Although this was not a denomination with which we were familiar, we decided to attend worship there the next Sunday. We found it quite acceptable and continued worshipping there for the remainder of our stay in Kansas City. I was asked to teach an adult Sunday School class and I also had the privilege of mentoring several young men, who regularly came out to Stonecroft early in the morning to meet with me. Edna and I made many friends among the people there.

Living in the Midwest was quite different from our experience in Oregon. During the summer, nights remained hot, so that bedding often became damp with perspiration. Thunder storms of enormous intensity erupted frequently. Rain fell in sheets, so that it became impossible to see across the yard. The sky turned yellow and continuous flashes of lightening ran along the ground. Sometimes tornadoes threatened, though none came near during our time in Kansas City. On fine evenings, fire flies flashed beneath the dense trees and flowers exuded a sweet perfume into the air. Chiggers lurked in the tall grass. Chiggers are almost invisible creatures that pierce the skin and cause intense itching. Mr. Duff used to say that the ecstasy of scratching a chigger bite exceeded all other sensations. When winter came, temperatures dropped to extreme lows. Snow fell heavily and hung around until the spring. Though beautiful at times, we found the Kansas City climate to be uncomfortable compared with what we had known on the west coast.

Alyson, Nicky, Jill and Andy all had to enroll in new schools. Andy and Jill settled in fairly well but the two older ones never did. Transferring from a small country high school to a large metropolitan area was bewildering. They made few friends and had difficulty adjusting to the different way of life. Alyson graduated while we were at Stonecroft, part of a huge graduating class, and was glad to find employment in a bookstore attached to the campus. Jennie returned from Capernwray and went to work in one of the Stonecroft offices. She later went to Ravencrest Chalet, in Estes Park, Colorado, to help prepare for a new Capernwray school, which was soon to open there. Nicky continued in high school but was very unhappy.

In August, 1974, Edna and I returned from church one Sunday to find chaos at Stonecroft. President Nixon had been forced to resign over the Watergate scandal. One might have thought from the fuss that

Stonecroft was closing down. The Watergate is an hotel in Washington where burglars had raided the offices of the Democratic Party. The burglary was bungled and the culprits arrested. The Nixon Reelection Committee was clearly responsible for the crime but an intricate cover-up was staged. President Nixon denied all knowledge of the cover up but eventually the Supreme Court forced him to surrender the tapes of all his White House conversations. These clearly revealed his complicity and with the threat of impeachment hanging over him he resigned his presidency. Gerald Ford took his place as president.

In September, Edna received word that her father had died. He was a commanding personality, with strong features and a set jaw. I remember being extremely nervous when asking him for Edna's hand in marriage. As a politician for many years, he was used to dealing with people. While mayor of the city of Reading he and Edna's Mum had been privileged to meet King George VI and also the present Queen Elizabeth. They had also traveled to Reading, Pennsylvania aboard the "Queen Elizabeth" for a state visit and had been presented to President Truman. It seemed strange to know that such a strong personality was no longer with us.

CHAPTER 11

Manzanita, Oregon

At the end of a year, I was invited to teach at Ecola Bible School in Canon Beach. I had been privileged to sit on the board that planned and launched this venture. David Duff, Walter's son, had attended Capernwray in England and had come home with a vision to start a similar school at Canon Beach, using the conference dorms and meeting rooms during the off-season. It had become (and still is) quite a popular center for young people. I welcomed the opportunity to renew my acquaintance with the Oregon coast.

Classes were open to the public and a number of friends from our old congregation in Rockaway drove up for the sessions. One evening, one of the couples drew me aside and said, "Did you know they were looking for a pastor at Manzanita?" They then urged me to apply. Manzanita is a small community a few miles south of Canon Beach, sheltered by steep cliffs that drop dramatically into the ocean. I knew Mr. Duff had watched the community for some time, believing it to be a potential Village Missions field. That weekend I was invited to speak at the church in Rockaway and Mr. Duff was present. After the service I said to him, "Calvary Bible Church, in Manzanita, is looking for a pastor. I know you have had your eye on it for some time. Do you think I should apply?" Without hesitation he told me to go ahead and I gave our friends permission to submit my name.

Soon after my return to Stonecroft, a letter arrived from Manzanita inviting me to accept the pastorate of the church there. It is a strange fact that in all our forty-two years of ministry, Rockaway was the only church at which we candidated. By that I mean it was the only congregation to which we preached in person before being called. All the others called us "sight unseen".

Edna and I sought the Lord's direction and felt that this move was within His will. Edna had not felt as restless at Stonecroft as I had. In many ways she enjoyed our brief tenure there, being free from the pressures of a normal pastor's wife. However, she knew my heart lay more in the pastorate than in our present situation and agreed to accept the invitation. Mrs. Baugh and Miss Clark were not happy about our decision and made their displeasure painfully obvious, but the decision had been made and in a short time the VM truck arrived to load up our belongings and head back to Oregon. We traveled in our old Volkswagen bus, which had been overhauled by the mechanic at Stonecroft. However, as we drove down the Sunset Highway, between Portland and the coast, I looked in my mirror and saw the rear wheel sticking out of its well on the end of its axle. I stopped, jacked up the bus and pushed the wheel back, hoping to keep the transmission happy until we reached our destination. Miraculously we made it, but only after several stops to repeat the procedure. Apparently the mechanic had installed the wrong half-shaft when overhauling the transmission and the axle had parted company with its seating, but the Lord was watching out for us.

Manzanita

Manzanita is a beautiful little community, nestled at the foot of the mountains and occupying its own sheltered bay. On summer days, when the sea is blue and the sun is warm, it would be difficult to find a more inviting location along the whole western seaboard. From a viewpoint, high above on the cliff top, the village looks cozy and compact, enfolded in its little bay like a cat curled up in its basket, and ringed by the scrubby pines that dominate that part of the coast. A few stores, plus a post office, dot the straggly main street, as it slopes down to the beach. There seems to be no soil, only sand, broken here and there with wiry grass. However, there must be soil beneath the sand, or the trees and shrubs that grow in such profusion would not survive there, but to the eye, sand prevails.

For the first week or so we were lodged in a house belonging to one of the church members, while builders completed construction of a beautiful new parsonage. This proved to be a well-designed rancher with large rooms. We settled in gratefully, happy to experience a brand new building with plumbing and wiring that actually worked. Back at Stonecroft this had not always been the case. On one occasion, when we flushed the toilet our contribution turned up in the next door neighbor's bathtub. This was not appreciated and a plumber had to be called in to correct the problem.

Our church, situated next door to the parsonage, was of fairly modern design and tastefully finished inside with pine woodwork. It was not as large as the new church in Rockaway but services were well-attended and the people were receptive and friendly. As in most country churches, we had our share of quaint characters but they helped to make our ministry there memorable. I quickly resumed my summer activities at Canon Beach. We were much closer now to the conference center, and less driving time was demanded by this activity.

Camping trip

During our summer vacation, we decided to go camping with the kids. We loaded up our Volkswagen bus and took off to Lake Cushman, in Washington. We set up the tent for the kids, while Edna and I bedded down inside the bus, having first removed the seats to make room. That night, Edna and Nicky were both taken sick. Also, torrential rain fell and soon found its way into the tent, making it necessary for us to pack up and return home prematurely. Everyone crowded into the bus while I braved the weather to demolish our camp. Very damp, we made our way home to Manzanita, where Edna and Nicky went straight to bed.

We had not been home long before there was a knock at the door. I opened it to find a young man standing there seeking counsel. He explained that his marriage was in trouble and that he and his wife needed urgent help. I talked with him for quite a while and set up some future appointments. I also invited them to church. They began attending services and it soon became apparent where their trouble lay. They had two small children who always seemed unhappy and crying. It seemed that the parents had no control over them. Instead of the parents controlling them, they controlled the parents -- with disastrous effect. Edna drew the mother aside and impressed upon her that she and her husband had to take control of their family. The absence of boundaries, and the children's consequent lack of security, was primarily responsible for their unhappy state.

The young mother listened to Edna's advice and immediately put it into practice. The parents reestablished their place of authority over the children and as if by magic the children's behavior changed. Within a short period they were happily playing together and the parents' relationship with one another was healed. It was one of the most outstanding transformations we had seen, yet the key had been so simple. God's prescription for a happy family certainly works! Eventually the couple enrolled in Bible School, with a view to entering Christian service.

The rain and the sickness that had spoiled our camping trip had seemed to be a disaster at the time, yet had we not returned when we did we may have missed the opportunity to help this couple heal their marriage. With God there are no coincidences; only appointments.

Problems

There were two factors that marred the happiness of our new pastorate. One was the violent opposition to it by the pastor in Rockaway. He was afraid that our presence up the coast, would damage his own ministry. In fact, it did not harm him because we were far enough away not to draw members of his congregation to Manzanita. However, our initial arrival caused quite a commotion because he complained to all who would listen and some took up his grievance. Eventually I was able to visit him and put his fears to rest. Although our relationship never became close, his antagonism eventually subsided and we were able to live in "peaceful co-existence". In fact, I was later invited to speak at his church on the occasion of their anniversary.

The other negative factor had to do with our relationship with the mission. One day we received a letter from our supporting church in Milwaukee, expressing surprise that their support check had been returned by Stonecroft with a note to say we were no longer serving with Village Missions. Nobody had informed us of this fact and Mr. Duff had given his personal approval to our applying for the pastorate at Manzanita. Severance from the mission also indicated that our health insurance had been terminated without our knowledge. We made an appointment with Mr. Duff and went to visit him at his home at Dallas. We told him we felt betrayed, since we had gone to Manzaita in good faith, and with his blessing. He avoided giving us a clear answer but it soon became clear that the decision had come directly from Mrs. Baugh and Miss Clark, who were peeved by our departure from Stonecroft. Apparently their action had amounted to a form of retribution. This was very hurtful because Village Missions had been our life since 1962 and we had looked upon the Duffs almost as family.

This last event made a deep impression upon us. We had often said that were it not for our association with Village Missions, we would probably return to England. Our roots were still there -- all our family and many friends. Now we found ourselves separated from the mission and our tie to the country was decidedly loosened.

Seed-Time Ministries

Good things did happen at Manzanita. It was there that our radio ministry "came of age". Up until this point it had no name or organization but was simply a private radio outreach that I maintained. Just before leaving Stonecroft, we had paid a visit to Edna's sister in Milwaukee. One afternoon I had sat quietly in the bedroom there and thought out the future of this ministry. I was reading Mark chapter 4, about the seed and the soils. Verse 14 says: "The sower sows the Word". That is what I was doing on the radio. I was sowing the seed of God's Word. Then in John 4:36-37, Jesus said: "He who reaps receives wages, and gathers fruit unto life eternal: that both he who sows and he who reaps may rejoice together. 37 And herein is that saying true, One sows, and another reaps." I would not have the privilege of actually seeing men and women come to Christ, but I could sow the seed and trust the Lord to make it fruitful. It was then the idea of "Seed-Time Ministries" came to me.

On July 16th, 1974, Edna and I met with an attorney in a nearby town and incorporated the ministry as "Seed-Time Ministries, Inc." A board was formed and Jennie became our first official secretary. Six days later we were registered as a nonprofit corporation with the State of Oregon. The US Treasury Department gave us 509 (a) (1) tax-exempt status soon afterwards.

In those early days, all recordings were made on reel-to-reel machines. I installed two turntables to provide music for the opening and close of each program. The records had to be cued and started at just the right time to sound professional. Cassette tapes were also becoming popular, making it easy to reproduce and send recordings through the mail. Their quality was still not good enough to send to radio stations but soon Bible studies on cassettes were being sent out in increasing numbers to private individuals who requested them.

Though brief, the Lord blessed our time at Manzanita. The people responded well and numbers increased. Nicky and Jill were happy to return to their old high school and soon became deeply involved. Alyson found employment caring for an elderly woman who was unable to look after herself due to a handicap that kept her bedridden. She was a sweet Christian lady and Ally became quite attached to her. Ally has commented since that her charge's calm attitude in the face of such adversity made a lasting impression upon her.

The Lord's Guidance

Throughout our ministry the Lord continued to give us indications that He was controlling our movements. There was an occasion when I was due to speak at a meeting in Portland. It was some years since we had lived in the Portland area and I was unfamiliar with the changes made to the city's road system. When I attempted to take the turn I remembered led to the meeting place, I was confronted instead by a concrete overpass that barred my way. I drove around, trying to find a route across the freeway but was unsuccessful. Recognizing that I would be late for the meeting, I prayed that the Lord would show me a way through the barrier. Almost immediately the car stalled and although I tried repeatedly (desperately) to start it, it remained dead. I happened to be outside a gas station and so I left the car in the care of a mechanic and called a taxi. The taxi got me to the meeting on time and everything went smoothly. After the meeting I took another taxi back to the gas station to see how my car was getting on. The mechanic greeted me with a puzzled look and said, "There was nothing wrong with your car, sir. It started up immediately without any problem!" I realized that the Lord had engineered the car's failure in order to get me to the meeting on time.

One moonlit night during our stay in Manzanita I was taking the dog for his walk. The Vietnam war had just come to an end, with a humiliating defeat for the US (politically if not militarily), and it seemed that such a high price had been paid. It reminded me of the battle between God and Satan. I remember stopping and praying out loud, "Lord, I don't know how long I have left on this earth, but in what time I have, would you please enable me to do as much damage to the enemy as possible?" I had no idea how this might be achieved, and I heard no reply, but as I returned to the house I felt that the Lord had heard me. A strange peace fell over me and I sensed a feeling of wellbeing.

Later that summer, Dr. Hunter was scheduled to speak at Canon Beach. As usual, I led the singing for him and during the week he and Mrs. Hunter visited with us in our home. I picked them up at the conference center and as I was driving them to Manzanita, Mrs. Hunter, who was knitting in the back seat, suddenly said, "Ashley, how would you like to go back to England?" I nearly drove off the road! How did the Hunters know about our thoughts of returning home? They didn't, of course, but God did and He was working things out according to His purpose. The very desire that had been growing in our hearts was His doing. Mrs.

Hunter then told us that they knew of a church in Ilfracombe, Devon, that was seeking a pastor and they felt we would fit perfectly there.

We had heard of Ilfracombe many times because in the past it had been a favorite vacation town. Before and during the war, when trains were the principle means of travel, people went in large numbers to the seaside for their summer holidays. Ilfracombe had been a favorite destination. After the war, when cars superceded the train and travel to the continent became fashionable, the old resorts like Ilfracombe, with their many hotels and guest houses, fell from grace. Instead of the bustling centers they once were, they became quiet and sleepy. Many visitors still visited during the summer months but in nothing like the old numbers. The idea of living in Ilfracombe sounded attractive.

CHAPTER 12

Ilfracombe, England

The Hunters went home to England after their conference tour and told the church in Ilfracombe about us. They must have painted a rosy picture because before long we received a letter inviting us to send them information. They suggested that we include some tapes of my preaching and answer a list of questions they had drawn up, which we were pleased to do. A short time later we received a telephone call from the church secretary asking if there would be any possibility of our paying them a visit. I explained that that would not be practicable and he agreed. He said he just thought there was no harm in asking. He told me that a members' meeting was scheduled to take place shortly and he would get back to me. About two weeks later, he called again and told me that the members had voted almost unanimously to call me as their pastor. Nobody had voted against but one couple had abstained due to the fact that we had been unable to attend in person.

In view of our impending departure from the United States, it seemed inevitable that Seed-Time Ministries would have to be disbanded. We therefore contacted the various radio stations from which we broadcasted, explaining the situation and alerting them to our imminent cancellation. However, the Lord had other plans. At the last moment, John and Lillian Penner, a couple from Bakersfield, California, who were briefly visiting Manzanita, asked if we would consent to them taking over the work. We felt this was a divine intervention and gratefully consented. After explaining the workings of Seed-Time we arranged with them to pick up the equipment when they returned to California. We also hastily contacted all the radio stations and told them to disregard our previous notice. It was quite an undertaking for the Penners. We shall always be grateful to them for their kindness. Seed-Time disrupted their home and their lifestyle but they willingly accepted the inconvenience as a service to the Lord and under their leadership the ministry grew.

Alyson left for England ahead of us, having no idea that we would be following her so soon. She went to stay with my parents in Cornwall prior to beginning her course at Capernwray Bible School. When she heard we were coming to Ilfracombe, she visited the church there and sent us back a description of what she saw. It was useful to have her input and postcards in advance because they gave us an idea of what to expect when we arrived. We had never been to Ifracombe and apart from her contribution had no idea what to expect.

We considered our return to England to be a permanent move. We were convinced that God had brought us to the States and placed us in a ministry of His own choosing. Through our association with Village Missions we had received much blessing but that phase of our lives was now complete. Our severance from the mission seemed to indicate that our work in America was done and we were free to go home. The fact that all our children were returning with us was another factor to be considered. Jennie and Alyson were now twenty-two and nineteen years old respectively and might easily have entered into relationships that would have kept them in the States, but that had not happened and they were still free. They both decided to accompany us. Thus, we departed for England with many happy memories of America, and sadness at leaving so many friends, but considered our departure to be final.

As we look back, the Lord's hand in this phase of our lives was evident. A combination of circumstances, beyond our control and perfectly timed, made our decision to return home possible. First, the action of the mission in severing our association broke our emotional tie to the country. Had this not happened we would have been disinclined to leave. Second, the call from the church in Ilfracombe opened a door of opportunity. Without that, there would have been no point in returning. Third, the legacy left by Edna's father provided us with the financial means to make the change. During our fifteen years in America we had been home only once, due mainly to the fact that we had been unable to afford the fare. Seven tickets to London amounted to more than we could manage. Now, suddenly, all three hindrances had been removed and the way was cleared for our return.

We arrived back in England on September 10th, 1975. A hired car was awaiting us at Heathrow and we drove to my parents' home in Cornwall, stopping on the way for a preview of Ilfracombe. My induction service was scheduled for October 9th, giving us a few weeks of leisure before formally taking over our duties there. During this time we were able to purchase a car and eventually travel up the coast to our new assignment.

Ilfracombe town

Ilfracombe was built on the side of a cliff, overlooking the water at the point where the Atlantic Ocean joins the English Channel. The south coast of Wales could be clearly seen in the distance. During the war, the residents of Ilfracombe had a grandstand view of the bombing of Swansea, Wales, a frequent target of the Nazi war machine. The part of Ilfracombe closest to the water was very old, dating back to beyond the time of Sir Francis Drake, who recruited vessels along this part of the coast to fight the Spanish Armada in 1588. The remainder of the town was principally Victorian. There must have been a huge building boom during the second half of the nineteenth century, when the railway was brought in and the community became accessible to vacationers. The town grew to three times its original size and considerable wealth flowed into it.

Due to its position on the cliffside, steep hills abounded. One winter during our time in Ilfracombe it snowed and everything closed down. There was no way traffic could negotiate such hilly streets in the snow. The main street, though narrow, was busy. Stores of all kinds lined both sides and there was always a bustle of activity. Many housewives had no refrigerators in which to keep food fresh. They therefore shopped daily, stopping at the baker's, the butcher's, the grocer's and the dairy individually. There was one small store that might have been referred to as a supermarket but it had no parking lot, no plastic bags and nobody to bag one's purchases. Shoppers therefore carried their own shopping bags and visited the stores on foot. No matter where you lived in town, if you had no car (and many women did not drive) groceries always had to be lugged uphill from the high street to one's home.

Brookdale

Brookdale Evangelical Church, where we had come to minister, was situated a short distance from the ocean front. Built in 1971, it had actually been a split from the High Street Baptist Church. By English standards it was quite progressive. Apart from the main sanctuary, there were fourteen classrooms, a fellowship hall, a youth hall, a small bookstore and a gym. Such facilities were rarely seen in England during the seventies. There was a thriving congregation, an exceptional youth group and activities more characteristic of America than England. The sanctuary itself was a large rectangular building, with tall windows on either side. In front, a low, removable platform covered a beautiful tiled baptistry, while behind this, rising to a height of six or seven feet and extending the entire width of the building, was a white stone wall. The pulpit was built into the top of this wall and a platform behind it for the pastor and choir was approached by a flight of shallow stairs. Below the platform was a room used for board meetings and another, known as "the pastor's vestry". When preaching I was elevated several feet above the congregation, looking down upon them. This was a new and somewhat uncomfortable experience. However, in comparison with other British churches it was unusually advanced.

Taking over a new church is always a challenge. You know that everyone is looking at you and evaluating you. You know you will be compared with the previous pastor and (initially at least) either approved or disapproved on that basis. Some people will attend services out of curiosity, some will resent the change. Others (probably the majority) will welcome you. But no matter what the individual reaction may be, the first time you climb into the pulpit you know you are on display. You feel awkward and are conscious of every movement. Your voice sounds like somebody else's and the message (that seemed strong when you were preparing it) now sounds boring in your own ears and you wonder how it is being received by the people. It is then that the "still small voice" reminds you that you are there not to please men but to serve God. That enables you to recapture your composure and settle down to the task of sharing the truth of God's Word.

The induction service was more formal that the US equivalent. Several speakers delivered messages (one expounding on all seven churches in Revelation 2 and 3). After a hymn I was officially sworn into office and public greetings were given by various other pastors in the town. Finally, I gave a brief acceptance message and the service was brought to a close. It was a very satisfying experience and I felt solidly installed into the pastorate by the time it was concluded. I was gratified that my parents were able to be present, a friend having driven them up to Ilfracombe for the occasion.

The church had purchased a home on Broad Park Avenue as a parsonage and we looked forward to moving in. However, our belongings had not yet arrived from the States and so we spent the first week or so in an apartment on the third floor of an old Victorian house owned by two single ladies. Ilfracombe abounded with homes like this -- large and spacious, with three floors above ground. The ladies were both extraordinary people, full of character and goodwill. We soon grew to love them dearly. Their home, a favorite place for gatherings after the evening service, was situated at the top of one of the steepest hills in town, which gave us an opportunity to become acclimatized to the kind of walking we would be doing for the next five years.

Dartmoor camp

During our stay in the apartment, the annual high school/college camp on Dartmoor took place and we were invited to go along with the kids. Dartmoor is a National Park covering a large part of Devon. It comprises about 250 square miles of open moorland with a sprinkling of small villages, farms and river valleys. It is one of the few real wildernesses left in England. Although not mountainous, the exposed land is primeval and bleak. Hot days are frequent in the summer, but the elements can be unpredictable, with mist, rain and bitingly cold winds moving in unexpectedly. Prehistoric remains abound.

A good, modern facility was rented from the park service for the camp, which allowed all the kids to be housed in the same building. The wild, windswept vastness of the moor accentuated the isolation of the site. There was nothing but rolling hills covered with scrubby grass and broken by great craggy rocks, as far as one could see in any direction. Across the moor, some miles from the camp, the grim bulk of Dartmoor Prison rose. This was built during the Napoleonic wars and retained the depressing characteristics of that period. Nobody escaped from Dartmoor. I visited an inmate there once and was very relieved to step out into freedom at the end of the interview.

Near the camp building was an old cottage where the caretaker lived. As a mark of respect, Edna and I were billeted there, to afford us some privacy. At bed time we were given a hot water bottle and a candle to light our way upstairs. The bedroom was icy. To make matters worse, the bedding was decidedly damp, which accentuated the frigidness of the room. The kids, on the other hand, were in high spirits and seemed to be immune from the cold. Every now and again they would grab someone by the arms and legs and throw them, fully clothed, into the stream that flowed near the camp. Apart from the inevitable screams and splashing, nobody made a fuss about being dunked and we realized that this was a traditional activity when visiting Dartmoor! I never did discover what one had to do to be dunked.

The isolation of the site made fellowship around the fire in the evening more cozy and intimate. Spirits were high and everyone enjoyed the warm fellowship. In addition, one of the young men took an immediate liking to Jennie. This did nothing to make Jennie's arrival in the community popular with the girls but a courtship began there which eventually culminated in their marriage.

Once our few belongings arrived from the States we were free to take possession of our new home. It was a brick-built Victorian house, having the usual spacious accommodation. An adequate hallway, floored with colored tiles, gave access to two large reception rooms plus a breakfast room and kitchen. A staircase, bordered by substantial polished banisters led to the upper level, where there were three bedrooms and a bathroom. Outside was a small yard which opened on to a public playing field. This was ideal for Andy, who was then nine years old.

Edna writes: "Before leaving Manzanita I had prayed that we would have a large garden where Andrew could play. When I first saw the small size of the back yard I thought, 'I guess God didn't hear my prayer'. But when we opened the gate at the bottom of the garden I realized that God had done 'exceeding abundantly above', as He so often does. I asked His forgiveness for doubting."

One of the rules we regularly set for ourselves when preparing for a change of ministry was to never negotiate salary. We were serving the Lord rather than men and therefore trusted Him to supply our needs. In accordance with this resolution we went to England without mentioning money. It was nevertheless rather a shock when, upon arriving in Ilfracombe we were informed that our salary would be £124.30 per month. That amounted to less than $200.00 (under half what we had been receiving in Manzanita!) To make things worse, the cost of living seemed higher in England than in the United States, which diminished the value of our income still more. Nevertheless, we believed God had taken us to Ilfracombe and He would supply our needs.

It would be misleading to suggest that we found living easy during our time in England. Had it not been for the money left us by Edna's father, we would have been in real difficulties. With his help we were able to purchase items of furniture for our new home and to meet various other unexpected expenses that surfaced from time to time. However, despite our meager income we never went hungry. God took care of us, just as He always had. Not all our wants were granted but He never promised to supply those.

These facts should not give the impression that the folks at Brookdale were mean. There were times when they demonstrated great care and generosity. We still draw a small annuity that was initiated by the church during those years. The salary we earned was normal for clergy in England at that time and we had to adjust to a different culture.

Old houses are inevitably linked with the past. This was illustrated very forcibly one Sunday morning when we awoke to detect a strong smell of gas in the house. Downstairs the odor became stronger and we began to feel alarmed. A spark could easily have caused an explosion, to say nothing of the toxic nature of the gas itself. The mystery was that the gas supply was not connected to our house! How could our home be filled with gas when gas was not laid on? We called the gas company and a crew arrived without delay. They didn't enter the house because they knew there was nothing to find there. Instead, they unearthed the main supply out in the street. What they discovered was interesting. Gas was escaping from a crack in the main pipe and was finding its way along the route where a gas pipe had once been connected to our house, probably many years previously, before electricity replaced gas for lighting. The pipe had been removed but the gas had entered the building through the tiny hole where it had once been and had thus caused the crisis. The workmen soon repaired the break and we could breathe fresh air again.

Ministry at Brookdale

Outward appearances are not always a good measure for evaluating the true nature of things. This is as true of churches as of anything else. Not long after our arrival in Ilfracombe, underlying problems in the church became apparent. Through the eyes of a casual observer everything was fine. Congregations were large, the youth group was flourishing and the women's work well attended. Brookdale was well-known and well-respected over a wide area. However, we had not been there long before we realized there were deep problems beneath the surface. Obviously God could not bless while this situation continued, yet dealing with it was not easy. It took a considerable length of time to resolve but the majority of the board supported me. Eventually the problems were solved and the church was restored.

Despite the difficulties, our ministry at Brookdale was busy and eventful. The couples' club was a particularly gratifying activity. Meeting in various homes, the "young marrieds" bonded and learned valuable lessons about Christian marriage. Summer camps were also eagerly anticipated. For some years before we arrived in Ilfracombe the church had made a policy of renting private boarding schools in various locations. Empty of students during the summer holidays, these afforded excellent facilities for summer camps. During our time in Ilfracombe we visited Bath, Cheltenham and Winchester. Each of these schools had a different atmosphere but all offered comfortable beds, dining rooms, kitchens, gyms, swimming pools and playing fields, not to mention access to various museums in their vicinity, such as the National Tank Museum at Bovington and the National Motor Museum at Beaulieu. The kids loved these places, especially the tank museum, where they could climb on tanks of all shapes, sizes and vintages.

Another special characteristic of Brookdale was its ministry on "the Rock". This was a large flat rock on the promenade that jutted out over the water. After evening services in the summer, groups from the church would go down to the rock and conduct evangelistic meetings there. One person would stand up on the rock and begin preaching. Soon visitors would gather around and sometimes we attracted quite a large crowd. Various members of the group would volunteer to share their testimony and sometimes visitors would jump up and give theirs.

On one occasion, a visitor shared how she had once decided to commit suicide. She had not been a church-goer and knew very little about the Bible. However, a verse of Scripture she had heard when a child kept going through her mind. She could not remember where it was found but remembered it was somewhere in the Psalms. Being of a curious mind she decided to find it before ending her life. She turned to the Psalms and began reading at Psalm 1:1. Before she found her verse (toward the end of the book) the Holy Spirit had spoken to her heart and she had received Christ as her Savior. Another unusual phenomenon concerning the rock involved one of our own number who suffered from a serious speech impediment. She had difficulty stringing six words together in normal conversation. However, she loved the Lord and would sometimes jump up on the rock to give her testimony. When she did so she was able speak fluently and amazed us by the freedom she was suddenly given. Only the Spirit of God could have done that for her.

Family Affairs

Within a short time of our arrival in Ilfracombe, the girls found gainful employment. Jill graduated from the high school and enrolled in an hotel management course at the Barnstaple Technical College and Andy was enrolled in the local grade school. After a slow start Andy made friends with some of the neighborhood children and school became a little less traumatic. Classes were difficult because the curriculum and system of teaching were so different from what he had known in the States. He therefore found himself trying to catch up on all subjects, which added to his difficulties.

When God is in control, He can be relied upon to expand one's ministry, without human help or intrigue. My relationship with Capernwray Bible School was an illustration of this truth. One day I was introduced to Billy Strachan, who was visiting some friends in the church. Billy was the director of Capernwray Bible School at that time. He invited me to travel up to Capernwray and speak to the student body at their end-of-year celebration. Edna and I enjoyed the experience, especially since Alyson was a student there and we were able to see her in her environment, first hand. Before we left, Billy invited me to lecture at the school on a regular basis, which I considered a privilege.

The next fall, it was Nicola's turn to attend Capernwray and my first year of teaching there. It was fun to have her in class. Capernwray Bible School is housed in a neo Gothic mansion that looks like a castle, complete with towers and battlements. It dates back to the beginning of the Industrial Revolution, when the wool trade made millionaires out of merchants. It is an ideal location for a school. Surrounded by 165 acres of parkland, some of which are farmed to produce food and income for the school, it presents a romantic setting for the students. The stone fabric of the castle makes it rather cold but classes are held in a more modern building close by, which also provides accommodation for some of the students.

1976 was a special year because so many important things took place in it. The romance between Jennie and Colin (the young man she had met at the camp on Dartmoor) quickly developed and soon it became obvious that their relationship was destined to be permanent. Their wedding was set for September 25th, but in the late summer of that year Devon experienced one of the worst droughts in living memory. Weeks passed with no rain. The reservoirs dropped to dangerous levels and eventually the local authorities turned off the water supply to all private homes. Standpipes were installed in the street and residents had to carry water in buckets from them to their homes. When expecting guests for a wedding this was not an ideal situation. Toilets no longer flushed and baths were out of the question. We were perhaps a little more fortunate than most because the stopcock in the street failed to shut off our water completely. We could therefore run a little water into the bath (being careful not to allow anyone to hear us) and use it as a reservoir for washing etc.

In due course the guests arrived and the day of the wedding dawned. As the morning drew on, clouds began to gather and an hour or so before the wedding the sky opened and sheets of rain descended upon the parched ground, sending rivers of water down the hilly streets. In the midst of the storm the florist called to say the roses ordered by Jennie for the bridesmaids were falling apart and could not be used. Later he arrived with substitute flowers but they were the wrong color. He took them away and made some substitutions, which rendered the bouquets useable but not what Jennie had anticipated. After the wedding, Colin had arranged for a pony and trap to take them up to the hotel. At first it was thought this would have to be cancelled but they defied the rain and, shrouded by umbrellas, bravely climbed aboard and took their damp trip up to the reception. It was a happy time, despite the weather. Nothing could dampen Jennie's joy at becoming Mrs. Colin Webber and we have photographs to prove it! Jennie had waited for the man God chose for her and now she had found him.

In November, Alyson was given the opportunity to go to Italy as a nanny. A wealthy couple in Florence (Dr. and Mrs. Folonari) were looking for a resident helper to care for their children. It was quite an adventure for Ally to travel alone to a strange country, having no knowledge of the language or of the family with whom she would be living. She caught the Orient Express from London and changed in Milan for Florence. There she found her hostess awaiting her. The Folonaris proved to be kind and gracious, treating Ally almost as one of the family. The children also became attached to her. The family owned the Rufino winery and during the summer they spent time in their villa in Greve, Chianti, giving Ally an opportunity to experience the Italian countryside as well as the wealth of culture to be found in Florence. She returned at the end of her time with many memories and a fair knowledge of the Italian language.

About the same time, Colin and Jennie made a preliminary application to immigrate to the United States. Colin, a licensed plumber, made inquiries about continuing his trade in the United States. The wheels of government turn very slowly and by the end of the year not much progress had been made. However, they persisted and trusted the Lord to open up the way if He approved of their plans.

During 1977 Archie suddenly died. He was standing in the kitchen with Audrey when he fell and did not regain consciousness. His abrupt and totally unanticipated demise caught everyone by surprise. He had suffered from some seemingly minor problems but appeared to be healthy and strong otherwise. His sudden passing came as a shock to everyone. Audrey was left with the farm on her hands, which necessitated making hasty arrangements to sell the livestock and equipment. She then moved in with Mum and Dad, and cared for them until their own deaths several years later.

In the summer of 1977, we received a visit from Dexter Job, the builder who had so patiently presided over the building of our church in Rockaway. Hearing of Colin and Jennie's slow progress in immigrating he and his wife offered to sponsor them. He thought Colin would be able to find work in the States fairly easily. In fact, applicants had to have work available to them before receiving visas. The project was complicated by the fact that US law ruled that jobs must be advertised for a specific period in the local press before being awarded to people from overseas. If there were no takers, the immigrants could have them. Under those circumstances the kids' chances seemed rather dim but Dexter and his wife encouraged them and promised to set the machinery in motion as soon as they returned home. They were as good as their word. Fortunately, a big building boom was in progress at that time in the States, so that workers in the building trades could find work easily. Consequently, the job Dexter had lined up for Colin was duly advertised but not filled. The way was therefore clear for them to make a formal application. This was done and in February, 1978, they left England to begin their new life in America. Thus began a migration which, unknown to us, would not end until the whole family was living once again in the United States.

Our twenty-fifth wedding anniversary took place in June, 1977. Time is a strange thing. Twenty-five years seemed quite a long time then, yet we have now been married well over twice that time and it doesn't seem any longer. In fact we sometimes wonder where the second quarter century went! Perhaps more events are crammed into the first twenty-five years than into the second. Our own childhood, our marriage, the birth and raising of the children and the first wavering attempts to earn a living, all take place during the first leg of the journey. Generally speaking the second is spent maintaining what we have. The church held a little ceremony to mark the occasion and presented us with a clock, which still stands on our mantelpiece. In the evening Edna and I had dinner at "the Sawmill", a delightful restaurant down in the valley.

Jill was the next to leave home. Toward the end of 1977, she had complained of back pain. X-rays revealed that she needed surgery. John and Lillian Penner heard of her condition and suggested Jill might go to live with them in California. There she could help with Seed-Time Ministries and undergo the surgery using John's medical insurance. Jill was excited about the idea and we began to make arrangements. By birth, she was an American citizen, which removed any difficulties involved in her return to the States. She was cleared in record time and in March 1978, just one month after Colin and Jennie's departure, we saw her off from Heathrow.

Later that year, Nicky also decided to return to America. She had accompanied us to England as a minor but now she was twenty years old and was obliged to apply for a visa of her own. This took time but due to the fact that she had spent most of her life in the States and had gone through school there, a visa was issued comparatively quickly. In February 1979 we drove her to London airport and she also left our shores. We were now a much smaller family. With only Alyson, Andy, Edna and I in the house it seemed very quiet and empty.

In May, 1979, John and Lillian Penner offered to organize a Seed-Time speaking tour for me in the States. The Deacons agreed that it would be good for us to accept and on May 17th Edna and I traveled to Bakersfield. John and Lillian met us at L.A. airport and took us back to their home. They were gracious hosts, arranging for us to speak in many places, including a week at the Hume Lake Conference Center. We were able also to speak at Redland, where a much larger church had now been built on land in a different location. The little white building that had been our first church had been sold and was now used as a business of some kind. There was a sadness in seeing the scene of so many "first experiences" taken over in this way but we knew that God was not limited to buildings. The people were happy and satisfied in their new location and the Lord continued to work in them. Our tour took us to churches in California, Oregon, Minnesota and Michigan.

A strange experience awaited us in one City. We were due to give a television interview at one of the TV stations there. Having arrived at the station, we were ushered into a studio and settled into the set where the program was to be shot. The host sat down with us and we awaited the cue to begin. The second hand of the big clock clicked round the dial toward the starting point, when suddenly, moments before the program was due to begin, all the lights went out. It was so black in the windowless studio that nobody moved. We just sat there for a long time. Apparently, a thunder storm had struck and lightening had disabled the station. The interview never did take place. Time ran out before the power was restored.

Jennie's accident

One Saturday morning toward the end of August, 1979, we received a telephone call from Colin in Portland, Oregon. He told us that Jennie had been involved in a terrible car accident and was in the Oregon Health & Science University Hospital in Portland. She had been driving north from Canon Beach in a Volkswagen "Rabbit" and had hit a truck head on. The car was crushed beyond recognition but Jennie had been propelled through the windshield, over the truck and landed in the road several yards on the other side. Had she been wearing her seat belt she would not have survived. Her spine was broken in several places, as were both her legs and she was paralyzed from the waist down. People heading for the Canon Beach Conference passed the scene and took word to the center, where it was announced to the congregation there. Though the people did not know the injured person was Jennie, earnest prayer was offered on her behalf before she even reached the hospital. Her attending physician arranged for her to speak to us by telephone. She said, "Don't worry mum, if the Lord wants me to be in a wheel chair for the rest of my life, that's OK." We have always been grateful that a wheel chair was evidently not His plan for Jennie.

Our church in Ilfracombe was most gracious and immediately agreed that we should go to see Jennie. On September 1st, 1979 we flew to Portland and visited her in the hospital. She was in good spirits, despite her injuries, and was trusting the Lord to bring her through. The hospital had placed her on a Striker frame which revolved on its own axis. Every couple of hours she was on her stomach, looking at the floor. Then she would be turned upwards to look at the ceiling.

Jennie had been placed under the care of a doctor who was experimenting with the use of DMSO, a remarkable substance extracted from wood pulp. If administered early enough following an injury it effectively reduces the inflammation and swelling which cause compression of the nerves. It is also a powerful antioxidant that interrupts hydroxy, which kills the cells of the spinal cord following an injury. In addition, it has remarkable penetrating capabilities, speeding medications in their function. It was not usual to administer DMSO intravenously but the doctor believed it might reverse Jennie's paralysis. The strong odor omitted by the substance was noticeable as soon as one approached her ward.

During the time Jennie was on her face, looking through a parting in the frame, she discovered she could read her Bible if it was placed on a shelf immediately below her. She spent time in this way, turning the pages with the eraser on the end of a pencil. One day, the Lord gave her a promise that made a deep impact upon her. It was Psalm 116:6-9, which reads: "I was brought low, and he helped me. 7 Return unto thy rest, O my soul; for the LORD hath dealt bountifully with thee. 8 For thou hast delivered my soul from death, mine eyes from tears, and my feet from falling. 9 I will walk before the LORD in the land of the living."

That night, the Lord awoke Pat Key (our baby sitter in Redland) from her sleep and directed her to the same verses. When she saw Jennie next day she said, "The Lord has given me some special verses of Scripture for you". To Jennie's surprise, it was the same passage she had found earlier. She took it as confirmation from the Lord that she would be restored.

In her helpless condition this promise seemed rather dim. It is extremely rare for patients paralyzed by spinal injuries like Jennie's to recover mobility. However, Jennie clung to the promise and a huge amount of prayer was offered on her behalf. One day she discovered she was able to wiggle her toes. This caused great excitement on her hospital floor. Very slowly, mobility and feeling began to return to her legs and in time she regained partial control. The Lord was as good as His promise. However, Jennie's injuries were far from healed. The breaks in her spine still needed time and the hospital authorities, assuming that she would never walk again, had not set her broken legs. The bones therefore knitted together inaccurately, which caused all kinds of complications later on. To keep her head immobile, a halo frame was fitted, which necessitated shaving her head and drilling holes in her skull to accept the screws of the frame. Initially they got the angle wrong and had to drill more holes in order to correct their mistake. However, the frame, although uncomfortable, enabled her to get out of bed a little earlier than would have been possible otherwise.

I returned to England at the end of September but Edna remained in the States for another three months. Jennie was still in the hospital when Edna left for home in December. Alyson flew out to relieve Edna and remained with Jennie for some time. Jennie continued to improve and eventually was able to function unaided, though handicapped as the result of her injuries. It is a miracle that she is able to walk at all but God, once again, proved that He is as good as His Word.

1979 was special in several respects. Not only did Jennie have her accident but Jillian announced her intentions to marry. Sadly, we were unable to attend the wedding but on November 1st, 1979, the marriage took place in Oregon between Jillian and Sonny (Henry) Kinsey, whom she met while living in Hillsboro. She was 19 years old.

On 22nd February, 1980, my father died after a short illness. He was a gentle, patient man, always ready to help where he could. During his career he had risen to the rank of C.E.O. in the Ministry of Supply but for the last twenty five years of his life he had been handicapped severely by unsuccessful hip surgery that left him crippled and in considerable pain. Nevertheless, he continued to work in his garden, leaning on a crutch and digging with one arm. He succeeded in producing quite a show of dahlias despite his difficulties. His funeral service was held in the little local chapel, where space was so tight that a small door had to be opened in the wooden wall at the rear of the sanctuary and the casket passed through to rest on the tops of several pews. He was interred in the tiny cemetery not far from the chapel.

CHAPTER 13

Return to America

Early in 1980, Edna and I began to have premonitions that we might return to the United States. This surprised us because we had genuinely believed our call to England was final. It would be logical to suppose that thoughts of returning to America were caused by the fact that half our family now lived there, but this was not so. Both Edna and I felt the prompting came from the Lord. There is an unmistakable quality about conviction when God produces it. Sensing that the work we had been sent to do in Ilfracombe was now complete, we began to pray that if the Lord intended us to return to the States He would take care of the details. We wanted to make quite sure that any invitation back to America came from God and was not manufactured by us. At the same time we made a covenant with the Lord that if we received a call from a church in America, no matter where it was, we would accept it, trusting Him to allow only that which was within His will to come to us.

We also agreed that any return to the States would not a be viewed as a continuation of the ministry we had enjoyed in the sixties and early seventies. That chapter had been closed when we returned to England. If the Lord called us back to America it would be to a fresh start, an entirely new phase in our lives, unconnected with our previous sojourn there. We had no idea what form our return might take, nor for that matter, if there would even *be* a return, but we were content to wait and see what the Lord had in store.

Shortly after making these covenants we received a letter that frightened us. It came from the Church of the Open Door in Los Angeles, asking if I would consent to my name being put forward as a candidate for the pastorate there and requesting a resumé. The idea of pastoring a church in downtown LA was most unattractive to us, and the thought of trying to take the place of Dr. J. Vernon McGee after his many years of ministry at that church sounded like a recipe for failure. However, we had promised the Lord we would accept any call that came and so we dutifully supplied the documents that were requested. To our relief, no further correspondence arrived from the Church of the Open Door. Perhaps this was a test to see if we really meant what we had promised.

Surpise from Coeur d'Alene

Early in April a second letter arrived. This time it was from John Hunter. He wrote: "This package is going to come as a surprise to you! I am wondering if, and how, the Lord has been preparing your heart to read its contents." The surprise was that a church in Coeur d'Alene, Idaho was seeking a pastor and John had recommended us as candidates. Enclosed with his letter was a letter of introduction from Don Bennett, an Elder in Coeur d'Alene, the current church by-laws, a bulletin, photographs of the area and several papers giving general information about the town. John closed his letter by writing: "It is April 1st -- an opportunity to be a fool for Christ's sake!" We were indeed excited. A large map of the United States hung on the wall in my office and the first thing we did was to find Idaho and then Coeur d'Alene. We poured over the photographs and read the contents of the package several times. This sounded like a real answer to prayer!

The following weeks were filled with correspondence and long distance telephone conversations. It was exciting to learn about the church. The first stage of our negotiations moved quickly. A day or so later we mailed the documents requested by the church, together with some tapes on Colossians. The Lord's timing was evident because our package arrived in Coeur d'Alene on the evening of a scheduled Elders and wives meeting. They were evidently satisfied with the contents because they unanimously agreed to present us as candidates at the church business meeting scheduled for April 30th. The three weeks run-up to the members' meeting seemed to drag. It was a big step of faith for a church to call a pastor, sight unseen, from the other side of the world. We wondered if the congregation would vote for or against our call. All we could do was wait and trust. If this development was from the Lord, we had no reason to be anxious.

During the interval we arranged to take a vacation on the Isles of Scilly, situated in the Atlantic, about 28 miles off Land's End. This ancient group of islands have an atmosphere all their own. They seem to belong to a bygone age. Most of the people who live there are employed either in the tourist industry or in producing the millions of Spring flowers for which the islands are famous. In addition, many men make a living ferrying visitors between the islands. Cars are few and far between. Isolated in the Atlantic, the islands have been a graveyard for ships as long as records have existed. Jagged rocks and reefs have accounted for over five hundred registered wrecks, along with many others that were never documented. Divers still locate new sites and often recover artifacts and coins from ships that have lain on the seabed for hundreds of years.

Edna, Alyson, Andy and I rented a small house on the main island of St, Mary's. During the day we explored the islands and in the evenings we attended some of the many presentations that were made in private homes. These usually included slides of wrecks discovered in the waters surrounding the islands and lectures about the artifacts recovered from them. Along the beach all kinds of objects could be found that had washed up from sunken ships. During our visit the beach was scattered with pieces of china that had issued from a merchantman that had foundered some years previously.

A castle dominates the hill above the town and one day we were sitting in the lee of its walls enjoying the sunshine. Birds, so tame that they would actually hop onto our legs as we sat there, busied themselves looking for food. After a while, Andy, who had been playing on the beach below the castle walls, ran up holding something heavy and said, "Dad, look what I've found". The object he was holding was a canon ball, rusted by centuries of contact with sea water. I followed him down to the beach and there, wedged in the cliff we found two more canon balls and eleven musket balls. We had to pry the musket balls out of cracks in the rock with a penknife, where they had embedded themselves upon being fired.

By rights, these artifacts belonged to Prince Charles since he is the Duke of Cornwall, but we figured he had a whole lot of canon balls of his own and didn't need those we had found. It was a case of "finders keepers" and we walked back to our cottage with our heavy finds hidden under our coats, like kids who had just raided the neighbor's orchard. Research revealed that the castle was last attacked by Oliver Cromwell's forces in 1651. We therefore figured that the canon and musket balls were at least that old. They had remained lodged in the cliff ever since the battle. Then Spring tides had caused the cliff to crumble just prior to our arrival, revealing the "treasure" at precisely the right time for us to find it.

The members' meeting at the Coeur d'Alene Bible Church was due to take place on April 30th, while we were on the Scillies. We had been invited to telephone the day following the meeting (May 1st) to learn the outcome. That afternoon we all walked down to the telephone box in the town and, holding our breath, made the call. Don Bennett was excited on the other end and informed us that the congregation had voted almost unanimously in favor of extending us a call. We then had the fun of breaking the news to Andy that he was going to return to the United States.

Unfortunately, news of our intended return was bitter-sweet to Andy. Initially he was excited at the idea of returning to the States but as the time drew nearer to our departure, he found leaving special friends very difficult. Peter Green, a veterinary surgeon who had become a part-time assistant pastor at the church and Andy's dear friend, Geoff Burge, had become essential players in his world. Peter had taken a special interest in Andy, taking him out on his rounds and introducing him to all kinds of interesting things concerning the care and treatment of animals. Andy and Geoff had also experienced many things together. Our impending departure now caused considerable regret.

Delays

Upon our return to Ilfracombe from the Scillies we received an official letter from the Coeur d'Alene Bible Church confirming the congregation's decision. It seemed as if we were on our way but we had underestimated the talent of government departments for causing delays. We applied for visas on June 12th and received a letter back from the embassy explaining that several documents were needed before they could issue a "Minister of Religion Status" visa. We contacted the church and they promised to send the required documents without delay. For the next three months we heard nothing. Our letters were unanswered and our telephone calls were blocked. We could never get through to anyone who could answer our questions. Eventually, a member of the Coeur d'Alene church who had political connections decided to pull some strings. She approached a local politician, who in turn contacted Senator McClure and Senator Church, both of whom carried weight in Washington. Senator Church was at that time chairman of the Foreign Relations Committee. Her efforts worked miracles. Suddenly we received a telephone call from the US Embassy in London, asking if we could come in the next day! We could and did.

At the embassy, we were obliged to go through the same routine we had endured in 1959, only this time there was a marked difference. The waiting periods were far shorter and we were treated with extra courtesy, which contrasted sharply with the indifference we had received up to that point. The reason for this difference soon became apparent. Our file was inches thick, containing all the unanswered correspondence from us and from the church, but out from among the many letters came two red ribbons, obviously marking letters from Senators McClure and Church. It is surprising what a little pressure from higher authority can do to make things run smoothly! We left the embassy with our visas and at last all obstacles were removed.

Not wanting to upset my mother unduly, we had mentioned nothing of our plans to her while negotiations continued. However, one day during the summer she received a letter from Jennie that mentioned how great it was that we would soon return to America. The cat was now out of the bag and next time we visited Tregilders, Mum confronted us with the news she had received and wanted to know what it was all about. It was a tense and uncomfortable time but we managed to get through it. We would probably have been wiser to advise her of our plans from the beginning but we had tried to save her unnecessary stress, in case the negotiations proved fruitless.

We were excited to be returning to the United States but our anticipation was clouded by the fact that Alyson could not come with us. She had been of age when we returned to England and would now be required to file a separate petition for a visa. A polite but cool letter from the embassy made that clear. In view of this, Alyson enrolled for nurses' training at Exeter hospital. She would live and board in the dormitory but Colin's parents in Bath kindly offered her their home as a "home base". It was with sadness that we prepared to leave her behind, although we were glad she would have a valuable qualification once her training was complete. By the time we left she was safely established in Bath.

It was sad to leave the people of Brookdale, who had become such an important part of our lives, but eventually our farewells were said and we prepared to set out on the next leg of our journey through life. After checking in at Heathrow we boarded a plane for Seattle and settled in for the flight.

Coeur d'Alene, Idaho

After changing planes in Seattle we were soon on our way to our new home in Idaho. Landing in Spokane, we gathered up our belongings and made our way down the ramp to the lobby. To our surprise, upon stepping into the lobby we were greeted by a whole crowd of people. They had brought a bus and several other vehicles full of members of our new congregation to meet us! Andy was scooped up by the young people and carried off to the bus while we, after hasty introductions, were piled into one of the smaller vehicles and driven to Coeur d'Alene. After stopping briefly at the church, we were taken to Don and Anneke Bennett's house on Lake Fernan, where we enjoyed a pleasant meal and fellowship. Before long we climbed into bed and spent a peaceful night, thankful for the Lord's mercies.

Next morning we awoke to bright sunshine and a magnificent vista down the lake. Banks of trees on either side were reflected in the water of the lake, while the sun sparkled on the ripples stirred up by a soft breeze. It was an exceptional introduction to the area. The beauty of our new home was impressive. Anneke was a gracious hostess and following a pleasant breakfast she whisked us off to arrange for our new accommodation.

The church had arranged for us to rent a property on the golf links at the Hayden Lake Country Club. Everything was taken care of. All we had to do was sign the lease and pick up the key. It was a peaceful location. Tall pines stood like sentinels and the grass, meticulously tended by the maintenance staff, was as smooth as silk. The Fall was late in leaving that year. Each morning a white frost soon gave way to sunshine and the air became warm and pleasant. It was a most enjoyable environment in which to live while becoming acquainted with the area.

The church placed its van at our disposal for the first day or so, after which a church member allowed us to use a big blue Cadillac he had spare. This was quite the longest car we had ever driven. With its fins trailing behind and the long hood stretching out before, we felt as if we were riding in a boat. However, once we became used to it we enjoyed driving it around town.

Our first meeting at the Coeur d'Alene Bible church was a Wednesday evening Bible study. We looked forward to this with anticipation. A good number of folks attended and we enjoyed meeting many of the people who were to become dear to us during future years. We were able also to explore more fully the church building. In those days it was a simple rectangular building, with kitchen, fellowship hall and restrooms in the basement, and the church office, nursery, a small restroom and my office at the rear of the sanctuary upstairs. It was less advanced than Brookdale but the atmosphere was warm and we felt welcome.

Coeur d'Alene in 1980 was quite different from the way it is today. North of town there was nothing but fields. There was only one traffic light, one supermarket and one very small mall. To the west, the prairie (now rapidly disappearing under hundreds of homes) was all open farmland, as was the area between Coeur d'Alene and Spokane. In contrast to the fast pace of traffic in England, the town seemed slow and more content. The roads were wider and less congested. This more relaxed atmosphere came as a welcomed change. In fact, the streets seemed so quiet and wide after England that Edna, who until this time had never driven a car, decided to apply for a license. She received this a few weeks later.

Anneke arranged for a real estate agent to call on us and before long we were driving all over town viewing houses. Several times when passing our present home we commented that we liked the look of it but assumed it was not within our price range. In fact, we almost settled on a small rancher in the Indian Meadows district but Don, recognizing our inexperience in things American, came to our rescue and advised us not to close. He explained that it was not a good buy and we should be able to do better. We appreciated his concern and advice. Eventually it was discovered that the house we had admired was, in fact, within our reach and we agreed to purchase it. We had no idea that fifteen years later a new church building would stand on property only one block away, but God did!

Our container arrived in mid-November, unharmed and unopened. It was gratifying to see our things take their places in our new home. The familiarity of our furniture created a warm sense of belonging. However, once settled in a new location, life inevitably takes on a normal routine. No matter how different or attractive one's new surroundings may be, they eventually become commonplace. The novelty wears off and the routines of life claim priority. These routines are basically the same wherever one goes. During our time in London I passed the Tower of London every day, yet I have never been inside. At Rockaway, Manzanita and Ilfracombe we lived within sound of the ocean, yet we very rarely walked on the beach. So it is with Coeur d'Alene. People travel miles just to be here, yet we live our daily lives without paying much attention to the beauty around us.

More Family History

Five months after our return to the States we received news that my mother had died (April, 1981). She used to tell us how she was born in the year of Queen Victoria's diamond jubilee (1897) and how her dedication gown had little crowns embroidered round its border in honor of the occasion. She was laid to rest beside my father in the little graveyard at Amble. Both sets of parents were now gone and it was difficult to grasp the fact that Audrey, Edna and I had become the patriarchs of the family but that is the way life is. Each generation eventually takes its place in the senior role. One of the sobering things about life is that we can clearly remember our parents when they were still in their thirties. As parents, they always seemed to be "old", yet in fact they were decades younger in those days than we are today.

Unexpected blessing

In May, 1981, we were approached by a church member concerning the possibility of Colin and Jennie adopting a baby. This person knew of Jennie's injuries and assumed she would not be able to have a family of her own. Apparently there was a woman who was due to give birth very soon and who wished to give the baby up for adoption. We contacted Colin and Jennie and they were excited at the prospect. Next month the baby arrived and Jennie went to the Kootenai Medical Center to claim her. Jennie was very conscious of her difficulty in walking and feared that when the hospital staff saw her, her handicap might interfere with the adoption. However, this fear proved to be unfounded and Jennie left the hospital proudly holding her new baby -- Tarris Louise. The nurses even insisted on wheeling her out in a wheel chair like a natural mother.

Edna writes: "There is something very special about grand-babies. This little one being our first was no exception. Tarris was a truly beautiful baby and brought with her so much love, as each new arrival does. It was also such a happy time for Jennie and Colin. The Lord had restored Jennie to health and now He had made them a family."

Two or three weeks after Colin and Jennie took delivery of Tarris, Edna and I went to visit them in Portland. During our visit, Jennie commented that her tummy seemed to be upset. She felt nauseous over the smell of foods etc. Jokingly, Edna suggested that she was pregnant. The joke soon proved to be reality when Jennie discovered that she was indeed expecting a little one. Adrian Liam was born in February 1982, just eight months after Tarris. In August of that year there was another arrival. My namesake, Ashley Brian was born to Sonny and Jill. He was a beautiful little boy with fair curly hair. We now had three grandchildren, all born within fourteen months of one another.

1982 proved to be a milepost in the life of our family. Not only were grandsons Adrian and Ashley both born during that year but Nicola and Bradley Rowe (who had met the previous year) were married in October. As always, this provided a great opportunity for loved ones and friends to reunite. In addition, Alyson was able to join us, though she had to return to England afterwards. However, it was not long before she was able to come over permanently. Having now settled in the country ourselves, we were in a position to sponsor her. This involved swearing affidavits proving our ability to guarantee Alyson a home and support, in the same way Ray had done for us back in 1959 and Dexter Job had done for Jennie and Colin. Alyson came home with her nurse's qualification but with no desire to pursue the nursing profession.

Trip to Europe

Following the 1984 Christmas program we were surprised to be presented with a present from the congregation. It was an all expenses paid trip to Europe. This was an exciting prospect because we had always wanted to visit Switzerland and Austria but had never had the opportunity. No travel to Europe was possible during the war and we had been too busy and too poor to make the trip once the war had ended. It was therefore a most generous and acceptable gift.

In May, 1985, we flew to London and were picked up by the tour company. Our flight arrived quite early in the day and we were unable to check into our hotel until 2:00 pm. Leaving our cases at the reception desk, we wandered off to Oxford Street, fighting jet lag, and killed time looking around Selfridges. When 2:00 pm arrived we grateful claimed our room and decided to go straight to bed. We had to be up by six the next morning, so we set the alarm clock as a precaution before retiring. At six o'clock the alarm sounded and we dragged ourselves out of bed, feeling horribly tired. However, slowly, as we groped our way around the room and our brains began to function, we realized that it was six o'clock the same evening (rather than six o'clock the next morning) and we could go back to bed for another twelve hours!

After rising with no problem the next day we were flown to Hamburg, where the tour began. It took us to Austria, Switzerland, Italy and parts of France. We traveled through incredible mountain scenery, twisting, narrow roads and ancient villages. Most of the overnight stays were in scenic or historical settings, where we had opportunity to walk and absorb the local atmosphere. We toured the Italian lakes, the Alps and the Danube, returning home refreshed and awed by the majesty of what we had seen.

Immediately upon our return we were thrown into a whorl of activity because Alyson's wedding was planned to take place within two or three weeks. Ally had met Doug Wayman, who had grown up in the church, and they had become engaged. Now they were to be married. With the help of friends, all arrangements were completed on time and the wedding took place on June 8th, 1985. There is always a certain amount of choreography to observe when marrying one's own daughter. First, you lead her up the aisle as the father of the bride and then you have to leave her and become the minister. The question, "Who gives this woman to be married to this man?" has to be changed a little, since you wouldn't want to answer your own question, but with a little ingenuity it works out fine. The first time (Jennifer) was a little confusing but later daughters' weddings proved less awkward.

Also in 1985, Andy graduated from high school. First he took a course at a Travel Agents' school and then joined the Idaho National Guard, going through boot camp at Fort Benning, Georgia. Upon his discharge from the guard he worked for Empire Airways and in 1987 enrolled at

Ravencrest Chalet, a Capernwray Bible school in Estes Park, Colorado. He enjoyed his experience there and did well, going on to serve for a short time in a church in Aspen.

Our fourth grandchild, Katie Elizabeth, was born on May 6th, 1988. When Ashley Brian had come along, Jill and Sonny were living in Florida but by this time they had moved back to Coeur d'Alene and we were able to enjoy Katie from the beginning.

Answers to prayer

It is often in the little things that we see God's provision. Edna writes: "After the children were grown and married we claimed their rooms for guest rooms. At that time we seemed to have a lot of English visitors. We decorated and rearranged the rooms but realized we needed towels. While out with friends one day we dropped into the Goodwill for some odds and ends. There on one of the tables were the most beautiful towels of the exact colors I needed for each room. They were brand new, with sale labels from the store still attached. Of course, they were very much less expensive now."

"As many readers will know, our taste in decorating is traditional English. One day, Ashley needed to shop at a small plumbing and electrical store. As I waited for him I looked around the store and to my surprise, in a dark, dusty corner I found a pile of lovely flower prints - the type used for decoupage. They were priced at twenty-five cents each. I bought two and had them framed. A few weeks later we planned a holiday in Port Townsend, Washington. As we wandered around the town one day we stopped at a tiny store that sold household items and gifts. Some lamps and piles of lamp shades caught our attention, and incredibly, when we looked closer we realized that the panels of some shades were the very same prints that I had framed."

"I no longer believe in coincidence. I believe God, having created us, knows us through and through. He delights in pleasing us when we are walking in the right relationship with Him."

Church Growth

By the mid-1980's the congregation had grown in size and our church facilities became inadequate. It was therefore decided to build an addition on the east side of the existing building. Plans were drawn up, permits secured, a contractor hired and the addition began to take shape. The plans called for the extension of the basement as well as the upstairs, and provided a new entrance, with wide steps leading up to the lobby, six new offices and glass doors into the sanctuary. My old office became a library and I inherited a new one on the opposite side of the lobby. In the sanctuary the pews were rearranged to create a center aisle (mainly to please brides) while an additional parking area across the street was secured to compensate for the space occupied by the new addition. The project greatly improved our use of the building.

Not only was the church growing during these years but our radio ministry also continued to expand. Soon after our arrival in Coeur d'Alene, John and Lillian Penner returned the administration of Seed-Time Ministries back to me. They made the long journey from Bakersfield, bringing the equipment and records with them. They had taken care of things admirably and under their direction the ministry had grown. But for them, Seed-Time would have ceased to exist five years previously. In fact, thanks to their generosity (in both time and financial investment) it was returned to us in more robust health than when they assumed leadership. They will not know, this side of Heaven, how many souls were reached during their watch.

Our most significant step in the development of this ministry was the addition of a radio station (ELWA) in Liberia, West Africa, to carry our program, "What Does the Bible Say?" Results were immediate and letters began to arrive in large numbers from African listeners. At that time postage was cheap and regulations lax. Over the following years we were able to send many thousands of Bible studies on cassette tapes abroad. At one point we offered a Bible correspondence course in which many listeners enrolled. Their papers were corrected by members of our own congregation. This proved popular because it brought our people into direct contact with overseas believers. Sadly, after the attack on the World Trade Center, on September 11th, 2002, regulations were tightened to such a degree and overseas postage rates rose so high that we were forced to discontinue all African tapes and correspondence. During the first Liberian Civil War, in 1990, ELWA was destroyed by rebel troops, making it necessary for us to find alternative facilities. We discovered Pan American Broadcasting, which offered a station operating out of Equatorial Guinea. This had a much larger coverage than ELWA and enabled us to reach not only the West African nations but also those in the east and south. By 2007 our radio outreach included three quarters of the African continent, the Middle East, the eastern half of China, northern Ireland and thirteen stations in the USA. A conservative estimate would be that in any given week at least one million listeners tune in to the program.

It has always been a source of amazement to me, how the Lord has consistently provided the funds necessary to maintain this ministry. Radio time is expensive, as is postage and equipment, yet at no time have we ever lacked funds. Month by month, throughout the years of its existence, the ministry's needs have been met by the generosity of friends and listeners. For our part, Edna and I have never profited financially from Seed-Time. The Lord has provided for us by other means and we are glad, as we look back, that at no time have we ever drawn personal money from the Seed-Time budget.

Office Changes

Great changes took place in the office during the early 1980s. When we first arrived in Coeur d'Alene, the bulletin was run off each week on an ink duplicator. A wax stencil was first cut on the typewriter and any mistakes corrected with what looked and smelled like nail varnish, applied with a tiny brush. The stencil was then attached to a drum on the machine, through which ink was squeezed. As the drum revolved, ink was released through the tiny cuts made by the typewriter and emerged as printing on the paper. It was a messy business. Copies of typewritten documents had to be made with carbon paper placed under the original. Copy machines had not yet been invented. All my messages were typed on a typewriter and any corrections made either with a white correction tape, which obscured the erroneous letters, or with a brushed on "whiteout" that painted them out. Neither method was very successful but they were the best we had available.

The first computer I owned was a used model donated by a businessman who was a casual acquaintance of the church. It was a Commodore 64 with 64k of memory. "Windows" had not yet been invented so a rudimental knowledge of DOS (the script commands still operative behind the Windows operating system) had to be acquired before it could be used. I remember it had an old document permanently burned into its screen where the previous owner had left it running too long. However, it was an improvement on the typewriter because corrections could be made without the use of whiteout or correction tape.

In May, 1985, upon returning from our European trip, I found a brand new computer on my desk. A member of the congregation had presented it as a gift. This was a great improvement on the old Commodore and I soon became quite attached to it. Messages were produced far quicker and copies printed with ease. Over the years, of course, desktop computers increased enormously in power and efficiency. With the introduction of Microsoft Windows their use was revolutionized.

Several years later, the first copy machine was installed in the church office. This simplified life considerably by making the ink duplicator obsolete. Initially, special thermal paper had to be used but it was still a great improvement on the old system. FAX machines made their appearance about this time also. Eventually we graduated to a copier that printed on ordinary paper, which simplified life even further and the modern office was born.

Philosophy of Ministry

Year by year, the number of people attending our services increased. We did not rely on recruiting programs but believed that growth was entirely in God's hands. This cut across the conventional wisdom but I believed it to be in harmony with God's Word. God proved Himself faithful. People trusted Christ while sitting in the pew. Over the years, the church grew considerably, without any conniving on our part. I believe the body of Christ is organic, perpetuating and multiplying itself as its members walk in the Spirit and reach out to their neighbors and friends.

I believe the call and training of pastors is also sometimes misunderstood. Some believe that a man cannot be an effective minister unless he has attended Bible college or seminary. I question this, not because God has blessed our own ministry without it but because the statement is not confirmed by Scripture. As the Bible illustrates, God is able to train and anoint anyone anywhere He pleases. All kinds of study materials are available to those who seek them. The important question is not, "Have you been to Bible school?" but rather, "Have you been called and ordained by God?" When seeking a pastor, many churches mistakenly concentrate on a candidate's schooling while ignoring the question of whether or not he has been anointed by God for the ministry. This often results in heartache and damage, to both the pastor and his congregation.

Plans to Build

In the course of time, the church grew to the point when it became clear that we needed to build another facility. This was not a small decision and the Elders spent many hours discussing the pros and cons. A new building would obviously entail a complete move from the existing location and would involve the congregation in considerable expense. In addition, if we were to retain our name (Coeur d'Alene Bible Church) there was a clear limitation as to where we could look for land. At the annual business meeting the matter was presented to the congregation and received a mixed response. Some were for building and some were against. No decision was reached on that occasion. We agreed to pray for the Lord's leading.

Meanwhile two of our men had located a prime piece of land, within the city limits, and for some time had been speaking to the owner about selling it, but without success. Then, quite unexpectedly, he contacted our men and told them he had changed his mind and was willing to sell. The property consisted of about eight acres directly opposite the high school. The location could not have been more suitable. The matter was quickly brought before the church, the desirability of the parcel recognized and an agreement reached to go ahead with the purchase. Soon we were the owners of the land, which effectively guaranteed that we would eventually build. There were still a few members who felt either that the undertaking was too large or that we were quite comfortable where we were. However, eventually a great majority supported the venture and an architect was engaged to draw up plans.

Many meetings were held with the architect, who took great pains to impress upon us his skill and experience. He drew up some plans and made us a model but before we broke ground he filed bankruptcy and we were obliged to hire a local man. He soon demonstrated his greater reliability and talent. The building consisted of a central multi-purpose room (gym) with two wings, each with a basement and two stories above ground. These would contain classrooms, nursery and offices. The two wings converged on a large lobby. A new sanctuary, capable of seating about 950 people, was planned on the west side of the lobby. It was an ambitious project but the Elders and other leaders of the church believed the Lord would undertake if we stepped out in faith.

A promotional program, named "Forward by Faith" was initiated, allowing members of the church to purchase bonds. These would be paid back with interest. Donations were also invited. Response was phenomenal and at the end of the set period we were able to stage a celebration banquet, during which we thanked the Lord for His faithfulness. The banquet was held in a local hotel and many attended. It was a great time of praise and anticipation.

Several contractors bid for the job and the board eventually settled on one who obviously had the expertise and facilities to tackle a project of that size. Soon we had a ground breaking ceremony on the land and the big machinery was brought in. We watched the progress eagerly as a great hole was dug for the basement and forms erected to pour the foundation. Then the concrete slab for the gym was laid and finally the walls began to go up.

Regardless of the focus on the new building, family matters continued to take their course. In May, 1992, Andy and Jan were married. Jan is the daughter of Pastor Dick and Shirlene Hege, whom we had known and enjoyed for some years. Andy and Jan had a beautiful evening candlelit wedding, during which Andy sang to Jan. Very romantic. Jan's Dad and I shared the ceremony. It was a special time.

Prior to his marriage, Andy had been involved in several bands and ensembles and had occasionally led the congregation in worship. Consequently the elders asked him to begin developing the early service and in May 1993 the way was opened for a more contemporary style of worship to be introduced. This was not immediately popular with some of the older members but was welcomed by the younger ones. For a while, I led the worship and Andy backed me up. Then, gradually a complete change took place. Andy was first appointed Worship Leader in 1993, then Music Director in 1994 and finally Pastor of Worship and the Arts. Over the years from 1995-2008 he succeeded in developing an outstanding music program, as well as producing (along with author/director, Randy Adams) some full-length dramatic productions at Christmas and Easter.

The New Church Building

On Easter Sunday, 1995, we held our sunrise service in the new building. It was still incomplete but we conducted our service on the concrete slab that would become the floor of the multi-purpose room, in defiance of the cold weather. Afterwards we drank hot drinks in the "fireside room", though the walls were still only studs and a cold breeze blew through the open spaces. Despite the discomfort, it was exciting to be actually meeting in the building.

By December, the central portion of the building was completed and we were free to take possession, special permission having been granted us by the city of Coeur d'Alene. It was a major project to pack everything up in the old building and move it to the new, but many hands make light work and we had a ready supply of volunteers. Our first service in the new building took place at Christmas, 1995, with great excitement and gratitude to the Lord. The office wing had not yet been completed. We were therefore obliged to find temporary places for the staff. The Assistant Pastor set up his office in the north end of the lobby, the bookkeeper took over what later became the ante-room to the ladies' restrooms, the Youth Pastor moved into the unfinished kitchen, Andy claimed the resource room and I inherited the unfinished elevator shaft. The arrangement was not ideal but it worked and we were able to function.

Services were held in the multipurpose room for almost eight years. This was not ideal because the shape and height of the room made acoustics difficult to control. Chairs had to be set up before each service and taken down again afterwards. The platform was temporary and this also had to be dismantled and re-erected if the room was needed for another function. From our first meeting at Christmas, 1995, Andy was in control of the music program. He worked hard, against odds, to improve the sound. He recruited teams to help him lead the worship services and the general standard of the music steadily improved.

In July, 1997, our fifth grandchild, Joshua Trevor, was born to Andy and Jan. This caused great excitement in the family. It was a new experience to witness Andy taking on the duties of fatherhood and talking about his new responsibilities.

Throughout the two years following our occupation of the building, construction continued and the wings were eventually completed. Progress was slow due to the scope of the project and the high costs involved. However, in March, 1998, we had the excitement of moving into the offices. We had walked many times through the unfinished office wing, imagining what it would be like to occupy these rooms. With only plywood on the floor and studs for walls this was not easy to do, but now the time had finally arrived. Upon my arrival back from a trip to Israel, I was forbidden to look into my new office. Paper was pasted over the window in the door and an air of secrecy prevailed. I realized something was going on inside but was unprepared for what awaited me when I was finally allowed to enter. A cabinet maker in the church had meticulously dressed walls and ceiling with beautiful inset oak panels. It really was a beautiful office and although I was to enjoy it for only nine short months, I greatly appreciated the love, care and skill that had gone into creating it.

Retirement

At the onset of 1998 it was noted that my seventieth birthday would fall on December 27th that year and the elders reluctantly agreed that this might be a good time for me to retire. Some of the Elders had kept in touch with a young man who had previously served on our staff and since he was a known quantity, well educated and had always expressed a desire to take my place as pastor, considerable pressure was exerted to call him. He was actually called as executive pastor but came with the clear understanding that I was due to retire. At the end of 1998, I vacated my office and he moved in.

Retirement Celebration

On January 10th, 1999, a service was planned at the North Idaho College auditorium to celebrate our retirement. Unknown to us, all kinds of elaborate arrangements were made behind the scenes. It was a miracle that with so many people involved no word leaked back to us. As it was, nobody broke the curtain of secrecy. January 10th fell on a Sunday and after the morning service some friends took us out to lunch. Apparently this was part of the plan, to keep us occupied while last minute details were taken care of at the auditorium.

By the time we arrived the place was packed with people. We were ushered to our seats and before long Andy opened the proceedings with a song. So far so good. That was what we had expected. However, having called us up to the platform and sat us down in two armchairs, Andy suddenly announced "This is your life". There followed the most jaw-dropping sequence of events, in which a video of our lives was shown, interrupted numerous times by the appearance of people who had played important roles in our lives, and who had traveled from England and far-away places in the States to participate in the program. Audrey was there and Colin's parents from Bath. Kath Brown, one of the ladies with whom we had lived when we first went to Ilfracombe was there, along with others from the Brookdale congregation. People from Redland and Rockaway were there also, including Pat, our original baby sitter, now a village missionary in Montana. John and Lilian Penner had also traveled up from California.

Toward the end of the program, I was handed a cell phone to speak to Peter Green, my Assistant Pastor in Ilfracombe. I assumed he was unable to attend. During the conversation, we glanced up and there was Peter, still talking on the phone, walking onto the platform! It was a truly amazing experience for us, to be suddenly surrounded by so many people whom we loved and who had played such important roles in our lives. The chairman of the Elders and the new pastor then appeared on the platform, and after an aborted attempt to entice me with a rack of elk horns, presented us with a check to cover the cost of a trip to England. Peter said a few words and the event was finally brought to a close. The people were invited to a reception back at the church. It was strange to see folks from such widely separated periods and locations in our lives all fellowshipping together in one place. It was almost like a time machine, or better still, like Heaven, where we shall all one day be together.

The next day there was a grand reception at the Clark House, a sumptuous Victorian mansion beside Hayden Lake. It was a great time of fellowship for special friends in Coeur d'Alene and those who were visiting from afar.

Andy later gave me the file containing notes on all the meetings that had taken place in preparation for the event. Many people and many hours of planning had made it possible. It was Andy's crowning achievement in coordinating such a complicated production and in bringing it off so smoothly. The participants had to be contacted, air fares had to be purchased, motel accommodation booked, the North Idaho College auditorium reserved, members of the congregation, past and present, invited and the talents of many people nurtured and combined -- all to converge on that one gathering. He brought it off with professional acumen. Alyson was responsible for creating the slide show of our lives.

This involved clandestinely spiriting photographs from us, putting them all in order and then recording a commentary to go along with them. An energetic young lady in the congregation spent hours constructing an album in which many people contributed photographs of their families and wrote personal testimonies. It was a precious addition to the celebration and still holds a special place in our home.

Visit to England

In April of the following year we took our trip to England. This was an eventful trip in several ways. We had arranged to pick up a rental car at Heathrow and when we did so we found it to be a French Citroen with a left hand drive. This meant sitting on the sidewalk side of the car to drive, while Edna found herself in the middle of the road, where she seemed to face the oncoming traffic. After so many years in the States, it was difficult enough to adjust to driving on the left side of the road but this problem added to the difficulty. Bends in the road were particularly terrifying because we expected to meet oncoming traffic head-on. It was rather like being in America and driving on the wrong side of the road. The narrow width of many roads in England, plus the hair raising way in which English people drive, made our first day or so a nightmare. Later we grew more acclimatized to the arrangement.

Having extracted ourselves with some difficulty from Heathrow, we made our way first to Sonning, where Edna had consented to marry me back in 1951. It was just as beautiful as ever and still exuded that sense of bygone tranquility which we had loved so much in our courting days. One of the striking things about many old English villages is that generally speaking they do not change. A modern house may be built here and there but the tight gathering of ancient homes leaves little room for major expansion. If this takes place at all it usually does so outside the village, where there is more room to spread.

From Sonning we made our way to Woodley, where we stayed for six days and enjoyed visiting with Edna's sisters, Beryl and Barbara. There was a sadness about visiting this area because Woodley was one of the exceptions regarding change. Many of the places Edna knew as a child had now been covered with houses and shopping malls. The fields in which she once roamed had been swallowed up and a busy urban sprawl had taken their place. Quiet country roads retained their original names but were now wide arteries bustling with traffic. It is sometimes better to hold on to one's memories and not revisit old haunts. Nevertheless, while there Edna had the pleasure of renewing ties with some old school friends whom she had not seen for fifty years.

At the close of our visit we drove down to Wimbourne Minster, in Dorset. This ancient town held good memories for us because we had spent time there during our courting days. Nothing there seemed to have changed. We booked a room in the White Hart, on the town square, and spent a most enjoyable week exploring the town and the surrounding countryside. At the end of the week we headed down to Cornwall to see Audrey.

Audrey now lives in a small village called St. Kew Highway. It lies little more than a mile from the area where so many of my childhood memories reside. The farm she and Archie worked for so many years lies beside the Wadebridge road, and next to it is the house where our parents lived. Just across two or three fields is Rocksea Farm, where Archie was born and raised, and where I spent happy hours playing with his brothers and sister. The little stone bridge over the railway line is still there but the rails have gone now, leaving only a grassy track where the trains once passed. In the valley below, nestled in its secret nook, is Rocksea Cottage ("Mifs Rowe's house") which played such an important part in our early years, while high on the hill above the Allen valley, the ancient church tower breaks the skyline, just as it has done for the past eight hundred years. The sense of peace and tranquility, which always characterized this area, still reigns, the quietness broken only by the sound of a soft wind in the trees. The tiny cemetery, where our parents lie, secluded in its border of Yews, lies a little further down the Wadebridge road. The whole area is heavy with nostalgia. It was good to tread this "hallowed" ground again and reminisce about days long gone by.

We had arranged with Colin's parents to go up to York for a week at the end of our visit in Cornwall. Gerald had booked us accommodation in an hotel there. At the close of our time with Audrey, we drove up to Bath, where we joined the Webbers and then continued on to York together. The hotel was pleasant but the weather was miserable. Heavy rain fell most days and we were forced to run from shop to shop in order to remain dry. All in all it was not the most successful week but we enjoyed good fellowship. The highlight for me was a visit to the National Railway Museum, where I was able to sidle up to some of the great locomotives I had known as a child and touch their side rods and pistons. I don't think they remembered me but I certainly remembered them! We also paid a visit to John Hunter, who had played such an important role in our lives. He was old now, and confined to a chair, but his spirit was as bright and refreshing as ever.

The last two weeks of our English visit were spent in Bournemouth, Sussex. Peter Green owned a house right on the seafront there and placed it at our disposal. It was a most enjoyable time. Peter and his wife, Sally, came down and stayed with us for the last couple of days and then led us back to Heathrow via Windsor. This was a great kindness because we dreaded heading back into such a busy area. Peter knew his way around Heathrow and took us first to the place where we dropped off the car and then on to our hotel.

The Lord works in mysterious ways. Our journey from the States to England had been particularly uncomfortable due to the closeness of the seats. We had attempted to upgrade our tickets for the return journey at a travel agent in Wimbourne but had been told this was not possible. We therefore committed our return journey to the Lord and prepared for a similarly cramped trip home. However, two inexplicable events took place on the morning of our departure. First, we had been a little anxious about handling our luggage, which was heavy, but when the shuttle arrived at our hotel, the Indian driver jumped right out of his bus, grabbed our cases and carried them aboard. This was a pleasant surprise, which set us off on our journey in high spirits.

Arriving at the airport early, we asked the booking clerk if it would be possible to have the two seats at the rear of the aircraft. We explained that Edna had trouble with her legs and feet and this would be a real help. We also recounted how our attempt at an upgrade earlier had been refused. The girl was very helpful and gave us the seats we had requested. When the time came for us to board the aircraft, the boarding clerk said, "Your seats have been changed", which disappointed us, since we had been promised the two seats we had requested. However, to our surprise, upon boarding the aircraft we were ushered into the first class section and enjoyed a very comfortable journey home. Obviously the Lord had taken care of our need in His own way. The girl at the desk had had compassion on us and instead of giving us the seats we had requested, she had placed us in first class seats at no extra expense. We arrived home refreshed and ready to begin our retirement.

Y2K

As the century drew toward its close, official warnings were issued that the world's computers could crash, due to the fact that they were all programmed with 20th century dates and could not operate into the 21st. If this happened serious consequences would follow. Electricity, water, cars, aircraft, telephones, general supplies, everything involving computers could all fail. Consequently, the majority of people (including ourselves) laid by emergency stores of food, water and gasoline for the car. Heaters and stoves were purchased, along with stores of kerosene and bottled gas to run them. We, in company with thousands of others, had a generator installed. Then we hunkered down and awaited the fateful hour. As midnight struck around the world on December 31st, we watched the television screen, expecting to see everything black out and shut down. But it did not. Nothing happened. Lights continued to shine in Australia and Russia and communications remained open. When it came to our turn to hit midnight in the United States we again anticipated catastrophe but nothing happened. I checked my computer and it still worked. Light and power continued to flow and the new century sailed in without any sign of crisis. In one sense it was rather an anticlimax but in another we were greatly relieved. We all had nice stores of food and supplies with which to begin the new century!

Back in the Pulpit

The new pastor's tenure at the Coeur d'Alene Bible Church was fairly brief. He resigned in February 2000, after a term of a little over eighteen months, and I found myself once more in the pulpit. This was not an imposition because I have always enjoyed preaching. It was what God called me to do. Since I was filling the role of Teaching Pastor rather than Senior Pastor I did not move back into my old office. Instead I took a small room just outside the main administration block and did most of my preparation at home. I would continue in this capacity for the next three years.

Throughout our ministry, Edna consistently attended every service. During much of our time we held two services on Sunday mornings, and for several years there were three. Edna was present at them all, partly to support me and partly to make sure she would not miss anyone who attended. This kind of spirit is often missing today but Edna displayed a devotion that set her apart from the crowd.

More Family Affairs

In May, 2002, our sixth grandchild made his appearance. Nicholas Evan was born to Andy and Jan. All our grandchildren are special to us but due to the fact that the elder four had lived mainly in other parts of the country, we did not have the pleasure of watching them grow up. Since Joshua and Nicholas live right here in the same town it is fun to see them regularly and watch their development.

The next month our 50th anniversary arrived. On June 28th the kids had planned a very special retreat for the whole family to celebrate the occasion. We gathered at the hotel on Schweitzer Mountain, where rooms had been booked for us all. Then we enjoyed a gourmet meal at Ivano's Ristorante in Sandpoint, and returned to the hotel for the night. It was a very special time and we greatly enjoyed having everyone together. The family presented us with a beautiful hardwood bench on which there were two engraved panels, one bearing the date of our wedding and the other of our golden anniversary. It was intended for outdoor use but it now stands indoors where we can see it. Next morning, after a breakfast together at Swann's Landing, we went to our separate homes. It had been great fun and an occasion we shall remember for a long time.

During our retirement years, Edna has developed a marked talent for writing poetry. To date, six poems have been published. They are all written with spiritual themes and her motivation in writing them is to be a witness to her readers. A collection of her poems is included at the end of this volume in the hope that they will be a blessing to those who read them.

Following my retirement, the addition of new staff created a need for more office space. It was decided that the room occupied by (and actually designed for) Seed-Time Ministries was now needed by the church. The suggestion was made that Colin and Jennie might be approached concerning the possibility of creating a Seed-Time office in the basement of their new house. (They had purchased the house next to ours with a view to occupying it upon their retirement). They graciously agreed to the plan and a beautiful new office was installed at the church's expense.

Brad and Nicky have served Seed-Time for a number of years and since moving into the new facility Brad has transferred all my messages from tapes to CDs. This was a monumental task but he patiently worked his way through it and even made duplicate archive CDs to ensure against loss or damage. This was a great service. Very little new material is now being recorded and so the existing archives are becoming more valuable. Brad also produces all the radio programs and distributes them to the radio stations. Nicky takes care of the secretarial work.

The New Sanctuary

Once the main body of the new church was complete and paid for it was time to think about the final phase of the project -- the worship center itself. This was a major project. We envisaged an auditorium capable of seating about 950 people. The same process we had passed through in the first building phases was repeated. An architect was engaged, a building contractor hired and a program initiated for raising the necessary funds. Because of the large spans involved, the main skeletal structure had to be made of steel. This required the services of a builder who could handle that type of construction. The same builder who had erected the remainder of the facility agreed (and desired) to take on the final phase, and since he was well qualified to carry out the work, a contract was signed.

The congregation watched with eager interest as the work progressed. First the steel girders were raised into their places. It was amazing to see how they all fitted together precisely. The initial measurements had to have been 100% accurate or the bolts connecting them would not have fitted. Once the skeleton was in place, the fabric of the outer walls was erected and eventually the heavy equipment remaining inside was taken away in order to begin the interior.

Throughout the building process, Andy was the Owner Representative and along with the chairman of the Building Committee, took the burden of responsibility. Endless telephone calls and visits from the builder filled his days. The acoustics, selection and installation of sound and lighting equipment all fell to him. The excellence of what is there today is almost entirely the result of his diligence. Few realize this. The average member of the congregation imagines that it all "just happened".

The church lobby became the connecting point between the old and the new. It was completely remodeled, creating a spacious and attractive entrance area, not only to the worship center itself but to the rest of the building. Once the floor was installed and carpeted, the pews were brought in, forming a wide semi-circle with the platform at its center. The main sound board was installed downstairs and the technical suite located above the entrance doors. Huge air and heat circulating equipment was installed in the basement and heavy curtains hung behind the platform. Finally the facility was ready for occupation.

On April 6th, 2003, our grand opening and dedication service was held. It was an immense pleasure to meet in the beautiful new sanctuary for the first time. The arched ceiling, soft lighting and bright acoustics were such a change from the multi-purpose room, which, after all, had been built as a gym. There, it was difficult to avoid noticing the basketball hoops cranked up against the wall on either end of the room, or the fact that the rows of chairs inevitably got out of line once people sat in them. By contrast, here in the new sanctuary everything was neat and beautiful to the eye. I was very grateful to be still in the pulpit when this day dawned and to have the privilege of preaching the first message from the new platform. As I stood behind the pulpit I felt overawed by what God had done. After the confines of the multi-purpose room, the new sanctuary seemed to stretch for ever in all directions. We had been greatly blessed. I thought of the little pulpit in our first church at Redland, where our call was first fulfilled over forty years previously, and I marveled at what God had done.

Epilogue

Things we miss

We are sometimes asked if we miss England. The answer is "Yes, we do, but England has changed and we miss the things we used to know. Many of these no longer exist." However, there are several unchanging characteristics that still draw our hearts toward the old country.

First, obviously, we miss friends and family. As the years pass the number of these dwindles but family ties persist nevertheless. Second, we miss the simplicity of daily life in England. The usual frenzy fills the cities but in the country areas life continues much the same as it always has, with people taking time to "smell the roses".

We miss the climate of Southern England which, unlike that of Northern Idaho, is mild and temperate. An abundance of flowers blossom in the Springtime and continue to flourish throughout the Summer. Gardening is rewarding rather than frustrating. The flowers you plant *will* grow, without danger of winter kill.

We miss the sweet song of the Blackbird, Thrush and English Robin, and the mellow call of the Cuckoo in the Spring.

We also miss the history. Here in the American West, everything is so new. We miss the old walls and worn stones. We miss the beautiful parish churches, many of which date back to Norman times and manifest the evidence of a bygone age. Consecutive congregations worshipped within them for seven or eight hundred years and the tombstones outside bear silent witness to their lives, lived out in a world that has long since vanished. We miss the peals of church bells that echo across the countryside on Sunday mornings, calling the faithful to worship.

We miss the compact nature of English villages, where it is possible to live quite happily without a car. Shopping can be done on foot and everybody knows your name. We miss the old houses, with oak beams over the doors that threaten your head if you don't duck, the overhanging upper stories from which slops were once emptied into the street below, and the narrow, crooked streets that remain unchanged since the days when horse-drawn traffic was the only means of transportation.

We miss the narrow lanes and the "rights of way" -- public footpaths that lead the walker for miles through tiny fields, heavily endowed with wild flowers in the Spring, and accessed over worn stiles. We miss the great houses that are scattered throughout the land, where sometimes the same family has lived for hundreds of years. We miss the ancient castles that rise from the countryside as if they were part of the land itself.

From a more carnal point of view, we miss the fish and chips, that taste so very different from the variety obtainable in these United States. We miss the clotted cream that graces the tables in countless English farmhouses and the pickled onions that always accompany a ploughman's lunch in the local pub.

Yes, we miss all those things, but God has brought us to America, where we are surrounded by our children and grandchildren. That is more precious than all the old nostalgic memories. Flesh and blood are what really matter.

Finale

These memoires record our movements from birth to retirement. I wish my own forefathers had left their stories behind in writing but they did not. Consequently, the record of their lives and times, apart from a few tales passed on by word of mouth, has been lost forever. How wonderful it would be to have a record of the daily life and experiences of a Great, Great, Great, Great Grandfather for instance. It is our hope that this document will break the trend of silence and provide future generations with insight into the life we lived in the 20th and early 21st centuries. I also hope that those who follow us will record the details of their lives for the benefit of future generations, if the Lord tarries.

As we look back, God's hand has been upon us all the way. He has led us, provided for us and protected us in ways too numerous to record. We learned early from John Hunter, Charles Trumball and others that the Christian life should not be one of striving but of resting. It is not a matter of what I do for Christ but what I allow Him to do through me. Of myself I can do nothing. As John Hunter used to say, "The only person who can really live the Christian life is Christ". The key verse is Galatians 2:20:

"I am (was) crucified with Christ: nevertheless I live; yet not I, but Christ lives in me: and the life that I now live in the flesh I live by the faith of the Son of God, who loved me, and gave himself for me."

We therefore give Him all the credit for anything that has been achieved through our lives. From the beginning we have simply been the receivers of His grace and are humbly grateful for it.

CHAPTER 14

Edna's Poetry

"MOTHER"

I see her now, such gentle eyes,
Always there to soothe our cries.
So soft her touch, so deep her care,
So faithful, her presence always there.
The world today decries her place,
Puts her out in the market place.
The children are left to stay alone.
They live in a house - but not a home.
O God, reach down and open our eyes.
Restore our homes! Please hear our cries!

Published by The Fellowship of Christian Poets, Poetry.com and Noble House 2003

"A GRATEFUL HEART"

For all I see around me;
The sky, so blue and clear,
The beauty of the woodlands,
Each birdsong that I hear
That spring would follow winter
Was the promise that you made;
That sun's bright rays would warm the earth,
And flowers would bloom again.
For the summer and the winter,
For the sunshine and the rain,
For joyful times and sadness,
For happiness and pain,
I thank you, Lord, for all the things
You've brought into my life
For each new part reveals to me
Your wise and loving heart.

——————————

Published by Noble House 2007

"ENDLESS FAITH"

I need His faith, that lasts through all my days;
That carries me through times of joy and pain.
A faith that lasts, though friends may turn away;
When long-held dreams may fade into decay.
Faith, that sees past time and space, to worlds
Unseen, promised by the One who does not lie;
To those who through His selfless life still pray,
And truly believe.

————————————————

Published by Poetry.com 2007

"GOD'S PLAN FOR MAN"

How can we possibly describe
The wonder of Your plan?
That you would come to earth Yourself,
To rescue fallen man?
Your love unfolds before our eyes,
Your humble birth, yet so sublime,
Your selfless life for others lived,
Yet so few understood Your gift.
No man could bring about your death
Unless you gave permission.
You laid down your life for all mankind,
In complete submission.
But Satan could not keep you there.
The sacrifice completed.
The love of God, abundant still,
You're by His side now seated.
He placed you in your rightful place,
A throne above all others.
King of kings , of time and space,
Forever and forever.

"GREAT AND MIGHTY COUNSELOR"

Great and mighty Counselor,
Lord of Heaven and earth,
How can I exalt You
At your time of birth?
There's nothing I can offer
To my heavenly King,
But the heart He gave me,
Broken and crushed for Him.
All the wealth of kingdoms
Would not be enough
To pay the price He offered
When He came to earth.
Oh my heavenly Father,
How can I begin
To thank you for your greatness,
And let my praises ring?

———————————————

Published by Poetry.com 2004

IF ONLY WE COULD!"

If we could only hear
The holy angel voices
On that first Christmas night,
When all of Heaven rejoices!
If we could only sense
The lowly shepherds' joy
As with rapture they beheld
God's precious baby boy!
If we could only know
God's agony and pain
Of parting with His only Son
To wash away sin's stain!

Would we not His costly gift receive?
And value Him, with all our hearts believe!

"THE ULTIMATE ANSWER"

They came to Him impure,
unclean.
Men of wealth they may have
been.
Despair and fear now filled
their eyes,
Rejected by those who passed
them by.
Jesus alone would heed
their cry,
Heal their wounds and make
them whole.
It's still the same. He has
not changed.
Christ alone can save
the soul.

"THE COMFORTER"

God of all gods,
King of all kings,
You came to Earth,
Salvation to bring.
You came to me
In my sorrow and pain
Neglected, forsaken,
Yet You knew my name!
You drew me with love,
So pure yet so strong.
You showed me Your cross,
Your amazing plan.
Come, precious one,
In your sorrow and pain.
Open your heart
To the Lamb that was slain!

Published by Poetry.com 2005

"THE GIFT"

The gift is intended for all who believe.
Bought at a price that we cannot conceive.
Not a gift that at will we throw idly away,
But one that increases in value each day.
So rare is the gift that it cannot be bought,
But the way to receive it may always be sought
In God's Holy Book, that has weathered all time,
Yet throughout the years it continues to shine.
This gift that is offered to all of mankind
Is to savor God's love in the heart and the mind;
To know of His peace and be filled with His joys.
Oh, how much greater than earthly toys!
The price of this gift was the death of God's Son,
The only true Savior, the most holy One.
So pure and so sinless was His precious blood
That is covers our sins from the judgment of God.
What greater blessing, when life finds its end,
Than to witness the love of our most faithful friend?
The end of the race, both forgiven and free,
Free to embrace eternity!

Published by The Fellowship of Christian Poets
and Noble House 2006

BIBLE COMMENTARIES by Ashley Day

(verse-by-verse expositions)

EXPLORING ISASIAH

EXPLORING ROMANS

EXPLORING 1 CORINTHIANS

EXPLORING GALATIANS

EXPLORING REVELATION

WHAT WE BELIEVE AND WHY

Copies of these books may be purchased through the publisher (Authorhouse 800-839-8640), from Seed-Time Ministries, 5350 N. 4th Street, Coeur d'Alene, ID 83815, Tel: 208-765-3714, email: admin@seed-time.org, or from the website at seedtime.net.

Printed in the United States
124430LV00005B/103-123/P